19482
gardening

WARDE FOWLER'S COUNTRYSIDE

WARDE FOWLER'S COUNTRYSIDE

Impressions
of a Victorian Naturalist

_____

Selected by
GORDON OTTEWELL

Severn House Publishers

© Severn House Publishers

First published in this edition 1985
by Severn House Publishers
4 Brook Street, London W1Y 1AA

Illustrated by Ray Williams
Typeset by Nene Phototypesetters Ltd, Northampton
Printed and bound by Butler & Tanner Ltd, Frome

British Library Cataloguing in Publication Data
Fowler, Warde
Warde Fowler's countryside: impressions
of a Victorian naturalist
1. Country life – England
2. Natural history – England
I. Title
II. Ottewell, Gordon
942.07'3'0924   S522.G7

ISBN 0–7278–2052–4

Contents

Foreword

In a merit table of past British writers on natural history no one would dispute first place to Gilbert White. W. H. Hudson and Richard Jefferies, in both of whom there is a continuing interest, might lay claim to second place, but William Warde Fowler had a great influence on my father's generation: it is high time that we had a new selection from his writings, and this Gordon Ottewell has now supplied.

Warde Fowler ranged geographically farther than White, though not nearly as far as Hudson, with his Argentine background, but in his concentration on the village of Kingham, where he lived for many years and on Oxford where he was a distinguished classical don, he shows the same sort of local devotion as White, about whom he wrote one of his Summer Studies.

While this selection will be of greatest interest to readers who know Oxford and the Cotswold fringe, there is plenty in it for the lover of the English countryside and its wild life to enjoy and for the conservationist to ponder on.

Warde Fowler's primary interest was in birds and he constantly refers to the changes in their status that have taken place in the quite long period – roughly 1880 to 1912 – covered by the writings represented here. Today's reader will search in vain for corncrakes and red-backed shrikes, and will be fortunate to come on breeding stonechats and marsh warblers (one of Fowler's special studies at Kingham) but he will enjoy in winter great numbers of gulls which were very occasional in Fowler's day and, in the numerous gravel pit lakes of the Thames Valley, massive concentrations of wildfowl, including hundreds of Canada geese.

But Fowler was primarily a lover of the small song birds. In a surprising and original anticipation of Desert Island Discs he writes that he would 'wish to have some birds as well as books for my companions' . . . 'I would have little ones that come and go regardless of you' . . . 'I would have warblers, redstarts, flycatchers, or better still, the wagtails'.

Nor was he in any sense a 'twitcher': 'the occasional appearance of rare birds is not to me more pleasing than the consistent neighbourliness of common ones'.

Fowler's predilection for 'difficult' small birds like the warblers is the more interesting because of his poor eyesight and hearing. These handicaps only emerge occasionally, as when he confesses to have heard the treecreeper sing only once. Indeed, he believed that it sang very little. So great was his influence that the statement convinced my father, who had excellent hearing, that this was the case and he often called my attention to a singing treecreeper as something of an event.

As he seems to have enjoyed unrestricted access to the countryside round Kingham, it is interesting that Fowler found little of the 'real old sheep pasture' left and that in broad strips by the roadside or as the vegetation of a deserted quarry: which is more or less the position today. He also mentions the 'substitution of railings or ditches for hedges', but as something that had not yet taken place to any extent.

The writings assembled here span a most important period in the history of natural history; Fowler believed in pencil and notebook rather than the 'clumsy camera'; he thought cuckoos dropped their eggs into hosts' nests (a subject of controversy until the camera resolved it quite recently), but he accepted and admired Eliot Howard's observations on territory and was an early student of visible migration.

All this makes Gordon Ottewell's selection first-class

Foreword

reading, and I am glad that he has been able to find space for essays such as 'In praise of rain' and 'Bindon Hill', which show Warde Fowler's full range. I hope and believe that this book will attract the attention of a new generation of readers to one of the founding fathers of modern natural history.

Dr. Bruce Campbell, O.B.E., Ph.D.

Introduction

*'Once a man's curiosity is excited, he will always find
work to do, and work that may be really worth doing.
Wherever he moves, he will find himself saved from
that intolerable ennui that men feel who have never
learnt to keep their eyes open!'*

WILLIAM WARDE FOWLER,
'KINGHAM OLD & NEW'.

William Warde Fowler (1847–1921), Fellow (later Sub
Rector) of Lincoln College, Oxford, was one of the leading
classical scholars of his day and the author of numerous
books on ancient Rome.

However, he deserves to be equally remembered for his
writings on natural history, especially birds; his books on
the subject were among the first to stress the importance
of observation of the living bird, and did much to promote
popular ornithology in less-enlightened times.

Fowler's achievements as a pioneer among modern
ornithologists are all the more remarkable considering the
twin handicaps – poor eyesight and severe deafness – which
dogged him throughout the greater part of his life. Like
Gilbert White of Selborne, for whom he had the highest
regard, Fowler confined the greater part of his natural

history studies to the environs of one village, Kingham, in Oxfordshire, where he lived for almost fifty years.

His earliest ornithological writings deal with the city of Oxford, however, and he later made valuable contributions on the natural history of Wales, Dorset and the Austrian Alps.

But it is not only the content of Fowler's writings that account for their appeal. His work possesses a rare charm, humour and literary quality generally which endears it to his readers and remains as fresh and readable today as on the day it was written.

Keeping this selection of Fowler's nature writings within manageable proportions has been far from easy. It has not been possible to include any of his delightful descriptions of his adopted village of Kingham, or of the village characters he described with such sympathy and skill. His two volumes of stories for children, *Tales of the Birds* and *More Tales of the Birds*, are also missing from this selection.

Like Gilbert White, Fowler never married, devoting his life instead to dedicated teaching and quiet, though intensely demanding, scholarship. Natural history was essentially a recreation and he, as he always insisted, merely an amateur in the field.

'When I was beginning to notice birds,' Earl Grey of Fallodon wrote in his preface to *The Charm of Birds*, 'I found delight and help in Warde Fowler's *A Year with the Birds*. Here was a man whose work, like my own, lay outside study of Natural History. He had been doing for many years with birds just what I was beginning to do: he had found it a pleasant path for recreation. This book of his did, as it were, blaze a trail, which anyone with an inclination to birds could follow, and thereby be led to find much pleasure.'

Countless more have followed that trail since and it is hoped that this new collection of Fowler's writings will prompt others to do likewise.

Birds in and around Oxford

Fowler's first published writings on birds appeared in the weekly Oxford Magazine *in 1884 and he continued to contribute ornithological pieces until 1908. Some of his early work later reappeared in his* A Year with the Birds *and three of his later pieces were included in R. T. Günther's* Oxford Country, *a collection of essays published in 1912.*

The following selection from the Oxford Magazine *spans the greater part of this period and serves to illustrate both Fowler's engaging style and accurate powers of observation.*

The Birds of Oxford City (1884)

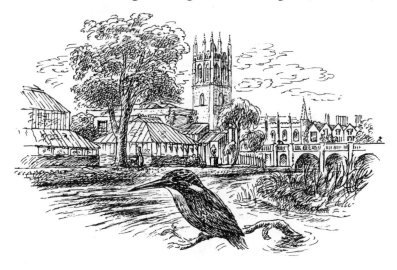

A Kingfisher in the Botanical Gardens

Probably no city in the kingdom so abounds in gardens and meadows as Oxford. It is, consequently, a paradise for birds; they find warmth, food and shelter in our very midst, and are safe from the barbarous depredations of ploughboys. Man in Oxford, though 'featherless, beakless and human' is friendly to the birds, or at least he is indifferent to them; and that is what they enjoy. The writer is perhaps the only man in Oxford who gives them any anxiety. He is apt, especially in Summer Term, to lurk in secret places with a field glass, and to set them a-chattering in some degree of alarm; but his habits are becoming inveterate, and they must by this time be accustomed to him.

I have seen a Kestrel passing over the Parks, a Kingfisher in the Botanical Gardens, a Lesser Spotted Woodpecker not far from the city, and further still in the country a very rare visitor – I may be allowed to mention him here – the Black Redstart. But the occasional appearance of rare birds is not to me more pleasing than the consistent neighbourliness of common ones.

I hope that all who are friendly to our birds will do what lies in their power to induce them to remain in their present haunts, by protecting them from air guns and catapults and from the youthful brigands who, as the Park-keeper tells me make inroads into the Parks at illegal hours in spite of all his watchfulness. Pleasant and exciting as it is to record the rare advent of some strange bird from sea or moorland, yet after all, our hearts incline most to the trustful little creatures who live among us the whole year round, and to the delicate travellers who come spring after spring, from distant Spain and Africa, to find a summer's shelter for themselves and their young in our abundant trees and herbage.

They find warmth, food and shelter in our very midst

An Autumn Walk (1885)

Fields hugging a great wood, where the woodpigeons feed

The age of walks is over. There was a time when both old and young used to haunt Bagley and Shotover every fine afternoon; now the once desired solitude is apt to become almost oppressive. Seniors still walk, but they do not often get far; they have too much to do. Their afternoons are now occupied chiefly in changing existing institutions and in projecting new ones; a form of recreation which in course of time becomes a passion, like the athletics of the juniors. The Undergraduate does not take walks, chiefly because he never acquired the habit at school. Since compulsory athletics came in, there has been something better to do than to ambulate aimlessly between the hedges, 'when fields are dank and ways are mire!' The average man is the better for his athletics, and as the public school system is not favourable to the acquisition of the first essential of an enjoyable walk – a sensibility towards the things around you, a quick use of eye and ear – it is not to be wondered at if he rarely finds himself outside Oxford, even on a Sunday.

Certainly the country around us is not inviting on an average winter day: there is a dull, silent languor about it, which weighs both on mind and body, and it is agreeably broken into on the river and in the football field. But on a bright sunny morning in October, it is more beautiful than at any other moment of our academic year. It is not that it is naturally more picturesque than any other bit of midland country in which meadow, water, woodland, are set together in quiet harmony; but the presence of this fair city, standing in the 'watery glade' far away below the heights on which you breathe a purer air, seems to give life and point to the landscape, as a gabled farmhouse puts a lovable reality into a long vista of chalky down or furzy heath. From Elsfield, from Stow Wood, and from the little wooded dell that nestles into the slope below it; from the familiar stile on Shotover; from the heights near Cuddesden, or from the Berkshire hills: from all these coigns of vantage the rambler turns instinctively to look at the ancient city in the plain, with a sense of love and solicitude, not often realised on busy days spent in her misty quadrangles.

I turned down the towing path on that cloudless Sunday morning, uncertain which direction I should finally take, but feeling that the river and the meadows were preferable to a suburban road. I looked for a swallow or martin, but there was not a single loiterer left, though two or three had been lingering a day or two earlier at Parsons' Pleasure. A few fishermen sat peacefully in the sunshine, unconscious emblems of patience under disappointment. Not a wagtail was there to break the silence of the water with its welcome note. In spite of the golden beauty of the trees, and the life that stirs the calm river at Iffley mill, I could not fairly rid myself of suburban associations until I reached Kennington, where I crossed the railway and made for Bagley wood.

Hardly a creature, man, bird or beast, was to be seen or

heard after I had left the village and gained the lane on the south side of the wood; yet there was much for living creatures to enjoy. Through the browned oaks in the hedgerow one could see into a paradise of mossy ground, chequered with fallen leaves, and lit up into green and gold by the sunlight cast from the last glory of the trees. 'We have not done even yet,' these trees seemed to say; 'we sheltered the first primroses for you when we were still leafless, and now our shadows are even more beautiful than the primroses, and our mouldering leaves will keep their roots safe and warm, however hard the coming winter.'

I turned into the footpath that leads to the little village of Sunningwell, through a series of well-timbered fields; fields hugging a great wood, where the woodpigeons feed, and the green woodpecker laughs at you from a solitary elm. I had them almost to myself; their only tenants were the cows, who seem to feel that it is Sunday, and lie on the warm turf at peace with all creatures, and the sheep resignedly submitting themselves to the impudence of the perched starlings. But the horses, amiably looking over the farmyard gate, feel the influence of the day more really than either cows or sheep. Who that has watched them in these delicious hours of their indolence, suffering their meek faces to be stroked by a stranger, or munching indifferently the handful of grass he has pulled from the hedgebank opposite, would have their day of rest disturbed, even in an age of agricultural depression?

How many of us know Sunningwell, nestling with its lichened roofs under the sunny side of Foxcombe Hill, hidden away in a silent corner? Above it the woods and hedges were that morning in the full blaze of autumn dress, from the deepest crimson to the faintest pale yellow, and brilliant with thousands of sparkling berries. As you mount the hill, the lane is sheltered by a hedge of glowing beeches, like the roads on windy Exmoor; and as the hedge ends, five-and-twenty towers and spires come, one by one, into view, from behind a foreground of burnished oaks. Away to the south there swims in the distance a reach, nearly fifty miles long, of that noble chalk rampart that stretched from Dorset to the Humber. Here the air is keen, setting both mind and body in healthy vibration, tuning them to the full sense of so grand a view. Far away is the hill where more than one battle was fought by Englishmen struggling against a barbarian invader; below you is the fairest city of the land,

Sheep resignedly submitting themselves to the impudence of the perched starlings

where men still struggle against subtler enemies. Surely it was gracious of the denuding agencies which washed away the chalk that once overlay our somewhat dreary clay and oolite, to leave us these Berkshire hills, from Cumnor Hurst to Foxcombe, to protect us from the dead flat that stretches beyond them to the foot of the great downs.

Crossing the main road to Oxford, I took the sandy track that leads along the very top of the heights towards Cumnor. This is the wildest bit of country near Oxford; here are gorse and broom and heather – yes, real heather if you know where to look for it; though while searching for heather and gathering a meagre handful of what was still left of its bloom, I was reminded of the waggon-loads of London children

An Autumn Walk (1885)

I once saw returning into the night of the great city with handfuls of grass in their pale hands. Here too are gold-finches airily dancing about the hedges and linnets on the furze; a pair of stonechats is still to be seen in a warm corner, and a kestrel sails overhead. Larks are singing everywhere; a few stray harebells enjoy the sunshine almost for the last time; the summer dies hard and breathes upon you even at the very gates of winter.

All the way down to Hinksey the eye is satisfied with fresh delights at every turn. The cottage standing by itself on a gentle rise, and sheltered by some half-dozen trees that are blazing with a depth of fiery colour more brilliant than that of any other in sight; the long slope of broken grassy ground above Childsworth Farm; the large farmyard with its huge oaks, the patriarch among which is little more than a gigantic shell; and then the deep yellow lichen of the village roofs below you, and nearing spires beyond. Here Eden must be left behind, and I am forced to wish, as I have so often wished before, that like the Oxford rooks, I could pass in one rapid flight over the mile of suburban defilement that lies between Hinksey and my old grey quadrangle, indifferent alike to railways and waterworks, to opening public houses, and to citizens in their best Sunday clothes.

Vere Novo (1888)

The Blackcap is the gentlest and quietest of birds

I write this on the very first day of this year which has been worthy to be called a spring day; one when the west wind does not blow, but breathes on you; when the grass is not only green, but full of light; when the songs you hear in the trees are no chance inspirations, breaking out each alone on a cold stillness, but reach your ear from the foreground and the distance, intertwining with each other without discord, poured out from hearts that have no misgiving, nor any need to be nursed by the shelter of a corner that the east wind hardly reaches.

East wind! Have we really felt and heard and seen the last of it? felt the last nip, and heard the last whistle, and seen the last snow? So used was I to snowflakes, that when the plane-tree that is my only sylvan neighbour in the heart of this city began to shed those little feathery somethings which have gathered outside my window, I could not but believe that it was snowing. There they lie in heaps, looking like malt, on the leads by an attic window; if you separate one from the rest, it looks an artificial fly for trout-catching. Our parks and gardens are full of exotic trees, and all our ordinary forest species abound; as you walk down that quiet bit of path in the Parks which leads *inside* the palings to Mesopotamia, you pass species after species of the great race of the willows, with labels fast disappearing, because no one takes any interest in them. There are wonderful trees in the Parks, of which I know nothing except what they look like; birches that peel a silvery pinkish bark in half a dozen different ways; flowering shrubs that are only just beginning to put on leaf, and deny you their acquaintance till you find an old friend in the blossom.

There is one tree, in a quiet corner though close to houses, which seems to have a greenish flower approved of bees and flies, and is chosen by the Blackcap as his favourite haunt. It was the 28th of April last year when I stood under this tree a long while, and listened to this choicest singer of all who now visit Oxford. 'He talks to himself,' I noted in my diary that day, 'in the intervals of each strain of song.' It seemed to me that he had to persuade himself that he must sing; for each time the real melody broke out, every feather seemed quivering with effort and excitement. This afternoon (7th May, 1888) I took a friend that way, and found the Blackcap there again. No doubt it was the same bird, for he was in the same tree; but this time he talked more than he sang. His mind was occupied by one if not two hens of his kind, and the three were restless and excited. Though he found his voice at last, it was hardly what it will be in a few days when he can sit on his twig with a cloudless mind, and try to make each strain sweeter and longer than the last. The Blackcap is the gentlest and quietest of birds, and when he sings in still air, and no rival is near, there is no voice in the trees that is quite so pure and touching.

A little Spotted Flycatcher – an almost voiceless bird – had chosen this same tree because it abounds with insects. It is wonderful how the same week brings the same bird each spring; almost to a day they are here, despite of weather. Last year it was the 4th of May when I saw the first

Flycatcher; this year it was the 5th. Last year the obvious Swift appeared on the 3rd; this year on the 4th. And not only so, but one sees them first in the same places. The Flycatchers come to the Cherwell-side in the Parks, I suppose because the flies, even on a cool day, are about over the water; the Blackcap, as I said, comes straight to the tree he learnt to love long ago.

The Swallows and Martins may be seen in numbers on the river in Port Meadow long before they have become familiar to the boating-man on the lower river. A very hard time they had of it this April. While those bitter winds blew, and insects could not come to life, or live if they were born, or find a warm corner if they lived, many swallows left the river, and sought shelter by the railway under the embankment that supports the bridge on the eastern side of the meadow. Here they *crawled* up and down, if one may say so of a creature that flies, showing their deep blue backs and even their chestnut throats to the looker-on as they passed almost at his very feet; often alighting fatigued on a bough or a bit of railing, or even on the ground, and looking altogether more like those poor captives who spend their days in walking to and fro in the Zoological Gardens, than the freest of all winged wanderers.

All these welcome signs of spring came this year before the true spring itself; before warmer breezes had (as Charles Lamb expressed it) melted your head, and let you feel that to sit for a moment out of doors was no longer flying in the face of Nature. We have had to wait long, but it is all the more welcome when it comes. 'Is spring really beautiful?' asks a young friend of mine, and argues that it is an *imperfect* time, when trees are not yet their true selves, and when neither you nor the birds know whether you are warm or cold. I am not going to argue the question. But when the first real spring day comes – a day like this, when you almost expect to hear the Swifts, those true birds of summer, screaming round our towers as the sun declines, there is at least something that gives new life and meaning to all things that live in fresh air, and that makes it hard to come back to musty rooms, where the dust of a whole winter lies unstirred by a breath of wholesome breeze from Cumnor Hurst or Foxcombe.

Back to musty rooms, where the dust of a whole winter lies unstirred

On Ducks (1889)

There descended with footing slow and sidelong a small company of tame ducks

Ducks seem to have an even more intense satisfaction in the material interests of life than any other birds; and the feature that chiefly expresses their placid enjoyment is that wide laminated sucking-instrument we call the bill. I never can forget a scene I once witnessed, when upon a ditch near Hinksey, the happy home of frogs, there descended with footing slow and sidelong a small company of tame ducks. One frog after another was seized, knocked against the bank and then quickly swallowed, his progress downwards being clearly visible from outside. No flurry, no excitement; only a quack or two of intense satisfaction, as a thirsty man might draw his breath and say 'good!' after a long draught of fine ale, and then to it again.

The domestic Mallard never quite equals the splendour of his wild brethren, and his bill and feet are always of a coarser build. This may be seen even in the duckling. Last summer the officer of the Humane Society brought me a brood of young ducks which had been found on a person of poaching notoriety, and asked me to bear witness that they belonged to a wild duck. With a friend, I sat in judgment on their miserable little carcases, and compared them with tame ducklings of about the same age; with the result that, though we were obliged to decline the oath, we felt morally certain, from the finer legs and feet, that they came from the nest of a wild bird.

The officer of the Humane Society brought me a brood of young ducks

There are certain feathers in a Teal's wing than which nothing in nature can be more beautiful. I am not thinking of the wondrous green speculum, but rather of the feathers which have the broad outer web pure white, each fibre being of such transparent pearly delicacy, and slashed at the upper end with a broad margin of velvet black, while the inner web is of soft cream-colour, crossed by wavy lines of deep brown.

A Ridge of the Cotswolds (1904)

We suddenly came upon a view

On a day of pouring rain and overwhelming flood, it seems almost hopeless to think of dry roads, clean air and the sight of plough teams no longer labouring gloomily over sticky fields. But at this moment I see in my mind's eye the 'red plowed hills' catching the sunshine, and I feel proleptically the breath of the sweet violets coming from the hedgebank. I wish to place my readers in imagination on a long ridge of hill where in a few weeks, these sights and scents, and many others quite as delightful, may be enjoyed by the bicyclist, or even the walker, in a day's expedition from Oxford.

This long ridge lies between the valley of the Evenlode and that of the Windrush. Take the train to Shipton-under-Wychwood, and from the station look up to the hills that shut out the view to the west; we may call them the

Cotswolds, and they are indeed the eastern escarpment of the whole Cotswold district, though just here they are actually within the county of Oxford. On the ridge a small round clump is conspicuous to the north-west; it can be gained best, not by following the direct road to Burford, but by keeping to the right as you enter the village of Shipton and making your way through Milton up to the top of the ridge. This clump can be seen from Cumnor Hurst, and we are by no means out of touch with Oxford when we get there; for on one memorable day, when the air was as clear as I ever remember it in England, I could see with my glass the houses on Boar's Hill, and the long line of the Chilterns far beyond Oxford. I could see too the other long line of the Berkshire downs with White Horse Hill, and beyond them again, the few straggling trees left on the crest of Martinsell.

Let us cross the field to the road which runs straight along the ridge to the north-west, at heights varying from six to eight hundred feet above the sea, open to all the winds that blow, and bordered by wide belts of true Cotswold turf, where in July the Marbled White butterfly abounds, where the flowers are those of the old down vegetation, and where the hedges are clothed with Traveller's Joy, rarely to be seen in the valleys below. Around us the land is now cultivated, but in the old days it was the fragrant pasture-land of the sheep belonging to the Cistercian Abbey of Bruern, on the Evenlode, of which only the fishponds are now to be seen, between Shipton and Kingham station.

Almost the first house you come to along this road has an enticing name, the Merry Mouth Inn, a corruption of the family name Murimuth. Adam de Murimuth, chronicler of Edward III's time, belonged to this family, which gave its name to the village below, anciently Fyfield Murimuth.

A mile or two further on, over the Gloucestershire border, the student of English History will find something to interest him if he keeps his eyes open. For a space he will find all hedges vanish, as he passes through cultivated patches divided by green balks, or meres, as they are called here. This is in fact one of those rare survivals of the old open-field system of cultivation, in which one farmer has to get to his strip over the strip of another, to his great inconvenience, as one of them told me on the spot. It might be worth inquiring in the village of Westcote why so awkward an agricultural system should have here survived to the delight of antiquarians.

Also visible from Westcote, and which cannot be seen from the high road to Stow, is one of the most historic houses in England, facing you from the other side of the broad Evenlode valley, not a beautiful house, nor an old one, but still the home of a great Englishman, Warren Hastings. It may be just visible among the trees which he delighted in planting; and the church of Daylesford, where he lies buried, is below in the valley. Daylesford is in an outlying bit of Worcestershire; but the next village, Adlestrop, where Jane Austen used to visit her cousins, the Leighs, is again in Gloucestershire – the gem of our villages, I think, and in summer a mass of flowers.

To the east again, we see a church tower which is in our own county, that of Kingham, my own home, the place of all others I love best in this world. There, some years ago, you might have seen a flag waving conspicuously in the breeze; all the tramps gazed upon it with satisfaction from these hills, for they knew that it meant eccentricity, and therefore in all likelihood benevolence, and they were not mistaken. Many a shilling have they won from the old Colonel who hung out the signal; who gave to the Oxford Museum a fine collection of Arctic birds, and left to the Bodleian his forty volumes of 'Log-book,' and in whose quaint companionship all my early walks on these hills were taken.

But we must make our way back to the main road, and set forth resolutely for Stow-on-the-Wold. The road begins to descend through woods, and brings us down to Stow station, where if need be we can end our day's walk and take train back to Oxford. But the bicyclist may well choose to make another digression here, and turning to the left along the great Roman road, the Foss Way, just beyond the station, pay a visit to the three 'water villages' as we call them,

A Ridge of the Cotswolds (1904)

Bourton-on-the-Water, and Upper and Lower Slaughter. Through each of them a clear trout-stream runs, right down the village street, picturesquely bridged, and in Lower Slaughter reducing the street to the size of a footpath; on each side are houses of the grey Cotswold stone, many of them old, with windows reminding us of College quads. I leave my reader to decide for himself which is the most delightful of these gems; I would only ask him, if it be spring, and he be on a bicycle, at any rate to take the footpath between the two Slaughters and enjoy the glory of the marsh marigolds as he walks along the brookside.

If we had gone straight on to Stow, we should have reached it by the Foss Way, which goes straight up the steep hill, after the manner of Roman roads, and passes through this curious little town, to descend again into the Evenlode valley on its way to the north-east. Perhaps even in those days there was a little forum where the town now stands, looking down on all the world; for Stow of course, means a market. Otherwise one does not see why even the Romans should not have taken the road over a shoulder of the hill, instead of over the very top of it. Anyhow, the fact that Stow is literally at the very top, and that if you were on the church tower you could see nothing higher but the sky, is just what makes it interesting. I well remember the first time I ever saw it; it was a Sunday afternoon in winter, and I had been walking with the old Colonel up and ever up, through the growing darkness and the snow. Not a soul was to be seen; street and house-roofs were snow-covered, and silence reigned around; it was like a deserted city. We had been toiling up over slopes where in 1644 Rupert tried in vain to stop the march of Essex, who had left Oxford to relieve the besieged Roundheads in Gloucester. All the way down through the big straggling village of Oddington the skirmishing went on, but it ended in Rupert's retreat, and this again caused the King to raise the siege and make that famous dash on London which was checked effectually at Newbury.

Once more let us set our faces to the north-west, and

leaving the Foss Way, keep to the road that still runs along the edge of this breezy bracing Cotswold ridge, rising even higher till it lands us at a point more than a thousand feet above the sea. And now, after a long stretch of desolate wold, we suddenly come upon a view which no one who has seen it can ever forget. The hills end abruptly; at your feet lies the whole plain of the Severn and its tributary the Avon; opposite are the Malvern Hills, in graceful outline, and beyond them, making you feel how small a country England is, seeing that you have but just left Oxford and the Thames behind you, are the dark ranges of the hills of Wales. Far to your right is Stratford-on-Avon; the village on the hill in the foreground, which almost hides it, is Ebrington of the Fortescues, where lies buried the famous judge, Sir John Fortescue, Chief Justice in the fifteenth century, the author of the Governaunce of England. The train that has just emerged from the tunnel under the ridge near Ebrington – the ridge that runs continuously from here to Edgehill – is hurrying down to Evesham, whose tower is visible even without a glass; it is the tower of the Abbey Church, where lies a greater man than Fortescue, Simon de Montfort, defeated and slain here just where the famous plum orchards whiten the land with their bloom each April. Beyond Evesham you can see the smoke of Worcester rising under the Malvern Hills, and with the glass, at least, you may see the cathedral whence Charles II surveyed the ruin of his hopes on another fatal day of battle. Further again, to the left is Tewkesbury, with its splendid abbey – another famous battlefield – and it is possible that on a really clear day we might see as far as Gloucester, if Bredon Hill does not hide it from where we stand.

Here our travels must end. It might be tempting to descend some hundreds of feet to Broadway, but in doing so we should be breaking the spell that binds us to Oxford; for once down here, we should find the water running to the Atlantic, and should see no corner even of our own shire. Let us turn sharp to the right at the Fish Inn – so named, I suppose, because there cannot be a fish anywhere near it –

and make for Chipping Campden, where the Noel Arms will receive us hospitably, and where the long picturesque street (in which there is hardly a house that is not charming to the eye) will make us wish to enjoy our meal out in the open instead of in a stuffy parlour. Then past the splendid Gloucestershire church tower, and the ruins of the old priory, we find our way to Campden station and an hour's run will bring us down the Evenlode valley once more to our own moist meadows and sunless streets.

Where the Noel Arms will receive us hospitably

Thoughts on Boar's Hill (1905)

Lying on the grass saying little

At last a beautiful Sunday morning! No fog, no rain, no piercing wind, but an air that even in the streets feels sweet, open and cordial. Before ten I am on Folly Bridge, and half inclined to take the sunny towing path, but the thought of free dry air on the hills prevails, and I face another mile of suburbs. My thoughts are already beginning to go back to the old days of Boar's Hill, and being alone, I feel just a tinge of melancholy in my enjoyment, but only such as we may all feel who have a long past to look back into. It will not vanish entirely as I mount the hill, for winter came upon us too early, and has already destroyed some of the pleasant things that used to greet the eye here. Where are the wild Geraniums that used to show in the hedgebanks, with even a bloom here and there as late sometimes as December? They are all killed by the hard frosts of October which have despoiled of their autumn beauty nearly all the trees but the oaks.

And as I approach the colony, where I have not been for months, new houses of all shapes and sizes tempt me to count them, but I soon get lost; and the old beech hedge, which used to remind me of Exmoor, has so many lacunae in it that it will be soon hard to decipher; and the linnets that used to dance about on the gorse are not here today, while human beings and bicycles are everywhere. The thought

The colonization of the hill is really due to the bicycle

comes into my mind that the colonization of the hill is really due to the bicycle, for without it the colonists could not speed down to their daily duties in the misty valley below. But I am not to quarrel either with the colonists or their machines; the air is putting me into good humour with them all, and in spite of all changes, how much is left that is grateful to a denizen of the damp city! The view of the spires, with the red oak-wood to the right of them, is still unimpeded, and the greater view across the plains to the seventy miles of chalk down can never leave us.

Thoughts on Boar's Hill (1905)

Nor is the peculiar Berkshire character of the hill as yet wholly vanishing. Boar's Hill with its appurtenances is geologically an island; but it is an island in another sense too. It is an insulated bit of one type of Berkshire country – the country of Scots firs, bracken, and gorse, with cottages of old red brick and tiled roofs covered with yellow lichen, and you must cross the plain and a good part of the Ilsley Downs before you come again upon such a combination of colour. The old cottages on the hill are not so obvious as they were, but all the rest is there, and neither on Shotover nor at Stow Wood, nor anywhere on the Oxfordshire side can I feel as I do on these heights that I am in Southern England. At Beckley or Forest Hill I am in the Midlands; here I am in the sunny South.

And the breeze today is from the south, with a little of the salt of the west in it to give it flavour as it converses with me. It must be a delusion, yet it seems to me that whenever I have been up here the breeze has been blowing from the chalk hills, and fondling me in just the same gentle way; not teasing me, but breathing on me, then ceasing, then almost blowing for an instant, then whispering, and again dropping. It never does this in the Parks or the Meadow, or if it does I do not gratefully recognise it; and the scent on it there, if there is any, is not the scent of sweet short grass, nor does it tempt me to shut my eyes and fancy that it is spring, and that I shall find the first celandine on the bank of the causeway beyond Hinksey Ferry.

The breeze will be here, and the views, and perhaps for a time the firs and the fern and the gorse; but no one can ever know again what Boar's Hill once was to one who now and again would selfishly seek a refuge there from his fellow creatures – from all but the chosen companion of a Sunday morning like this. My first companion in these wilds, as then they were, was a vigorous walker whose books on Roman society won him an honoured name in recent years. He had been the first of us to discover the hill, and he used to pronounce its name – he was an Irishman – with a peculiar tenderness that still lingers in the memory. But more especially I associate the hill with a young scholar, almost morbid in his desire to get away from his kind, who would linger with me about the slopes for more than half a Sunday, listening to the nightingales on the sunny side of Foxcombe, or lying on the grass saying little, and watching the red-backed shrikes on the fence in front of us. Whether in his day I had discovered the grasshopper warbler here I cannot remember, but there were years in which I never failed to see and hear it, in the dingle below the Fox Inn, or in the little copse in the hollow on the other side of the hill as you approach what was lately the golf ground. There are no happier recollections in my life than those mornings with this Scholar Gipsy, in the solitudes of Boar's Hill and Foxcombe; a village boy from Wootton might greet us, or it might possibly happen that the approach of a pair of undergraduates would cause us to retreat further into the wood, but as a rule we had it all to ourselves, we and the birds.

The spell was one day broken suddenly, but my Scholar Gipsy was spared that pain; he had gone to be a solicitor in London, and nothing could ever persuade him to visit the old haunts again. And though the world does not grow more beautiful, it is perhaps beautiful for more of us than it used to be. I will not allow myself to lament. Powderhill Copse is still untouched, and the fern under its oaks has put on a tinge of red which is simply indescribable; it may be that I have hit the one day in the year on which this wood is glorified beyond all others – the oaks still wearing their ruddy leafage, the sandy track glistening from last night's rain, and the sunlight there, but half subdued.

And so to Snow Bunting Barn – no one knows the name but myself; you will not find it on the ordnance map. Here, one bitterly cold day, I found two snow buntings feeding on the seeds of the hay. Day after day I came to visit them, and with a delightful confidence that is peculiar to the species in winter, they would come pecking round my feet. On the last day I had a plaid to protect me against the biting wind and snow, and this I tried to throw over them, thinking to catch one; they flew away for the moment, and then returned to my feet, as confident in my goodwill as ever.

From Snow Bunting Barn under the Hurst it is not far to the Cumnor road, and even here there are new houses and invitations to come and build. What will it all be like fifty years hence, and where will the Scholar Gipsy of that day find his rest? For that matter, will such a creature be suffered even to exist?

A Year with the Birds

A Year with the Birds, *Fowler's first book, was published by Benjamin Blackwell in April 1886, to be followed by a second, enlarged edition in the November of the same year.*

Originally appearing anonymously, ascribed to 'An Oxford Tutor', its popularity proved so great that a further, illustrated edition was brought out by Macmillans in 1889, of which reprints appeared in 1891, 1902, 1914, 1925, and finally in 1931, ten years after Fowler's death.

In addition to the four chapters on the birds of Oxford and Kingham reproduced here, A Year with the Birds *comprises chapters on bird life in the Austrian Alps during June and September and also a chapter on the birds featuring in the poetry of Virgil, on whom Fowler was one of the foremost authorities of his day.*

Many writers regard the first book as their favourite and Fowler was no exception. Towards the end of his life he wrote: 'In this little book, there is a certain quality of simplicity and honesty, visible both in the style and the matter, which perhaps is hardly to be found in any other of my books. I had something definite to say in every page, for I had made very careful notes about everything that I did notice, and my memory in matters so interesting to me was rarely at fault.'

Oxford: Autumn and Winter

The rod has given way to a field glass

For several years past I have contrived, even on the busiest or the rainiest Oxford mornings, to steal out for twenty minutes or half an hour soon after breakfast, and in the Broad Walk, the Botanic Garden or the Parks, to let my senses exercise themselves on things outside me. This habit dates from the time when I was an ardent fisherman, and daily within reach of trout; a long spell of work in the early morning used to be effectually counteracted by an endeavour to beguile a trout after breakfast.

By degrees, and owing to altered circumstances, the rod has given way to a field-glass, and the passion for killing has been displaced by a desire to see and know; a revolution which I consider has been beneficial, not only to the trout, but to myself. In the peaceful study of birds I have found an occupation which exactly falls in with the habit I had formed

– for it is in the early morning that birds are most active and least disturbed by human beings; an occupation too which can be carried on at all times of the day in Oxford with much greater success than I could possibly have imagined when I began it. Even for one who has not often time or strength to take long rambles in the country round us, it is astonishing how much of the beauty, the habits, and the songs of birds may be learnt within the city itself, or in its immediate precincts.

The fact is, that for several obvious reasons, Oxford is almost a Paradise of birds. All the conditions of the neighbourhood, as it is now, are favourable to them. The three chief requisites of the life of most birds are food, water, and some kind of cover. For food, be they insect-eaters, or grub-eaters, they need never lack near Oxford. Our vast expanse of moist alluvial meadows – unequalled at any other point in the Thames valley – is extraordinarily productive of grubs and flies, as it is of other things unpleasant to man. Any one can verify this for himself who will walk along the Isis on a warm summer evening, or watch the Sand-martins as he crosses the meadows to Hinksey. Snails too abound; no less than ninety-three species have been collected and recorded by a late pupil of mine. The ditches in all the water-meadows are teeming with fresh-water molluscs, and I have seen them dying by hundreds when left high and dry in a sultry season. Water of course is everywhere; the fact that our city was built at the confluence of Isis and Cherwell has had a good deal of influence on its bird-life. But after all, as far as the city itself is concerned, it is probably the conservative tranquillity and the comfortable cover of the gardens and parks that has chiefly attracted the birds. I fancy there is hardly a town in Europe of equal size where such favourable conditions are offered them, unless it be one of the old-fashioned well-timbered kind, such as Wiesbaden, Bath, or Dresden. The college system, which has had so much influence on Oxford in other ways, and the control exercised by the University over the government of the town, have had much to do with this, and the only adverse element even at the present day is the gradual but steady extension of building to the north, south, and west. A glance at a map of Oxford will show how large a space in the centre of the town is occupied by college gardens all well-timbered and planted, and if to these are added Christchurch Meadow, Magdalen Park, the Botanic Garden, and the Parks together with the adjoining fields, it will be seen that there must be abundant opportunity for observations, and some real reason for an attempt to record them.

When we return to Oxford after our Long Vacation, the only summer migrants that have not departed southwards are a few Swallows, to be seen along the banks of the river, and half-a-dozen lazy Martins that may cling for two or three weeks longer to their favourite nooks about the buildings of Merton and Magdalen. Last year (1884) none of these stayed to see November, so far as I could ascertain; but they were arrested on the south coast by a spell of real warm weather, where the genial sun was deluding the Robins and Sparrows into fancying the winter already past. In some years they may be seen on sunny days, even up to the end of the first week of November, hawking for flies about the meadow-front of Merton, probably the warmest spot in Oxford. White of Selborne saw one as late as the 20th of November, on a very sunny warm morning, in one of the quadrangles of Christchurch; it belonged, no doubt, to a late September brood, and had been unable to fly when the rest departed.

It is at first rather sad to find silence reigning in the thickets and reed-beds that were alive with songsters during the summer term. The familiar pollards and thorn-bushes, where the Willow-warblers and Whitethroats were every morning to be seen or heard, are like so many desolate College rooms in the heart of the Long Vacation. Deserted nests, black and mouldy, come to light as the leaves drop from the trees – nurseries whose children have gone forth to try their fortune in distant countries. But we soon discover that things are not so bad as they seem. The silence is not quite unbroken; winter visitors arrive, and the novelty of their voices is cheering, even if they do not break into song; some kinds are here in greater numbers than in the hot weather, and others show themselves more boldly, emerging from leafy recesses in search of food and sunshine.

Every autumn brings us a considerable immigration of birds that have been absent during the summer and increases the number of some species who reside with us in greater or less abundance all the year. Among these is the familiar Robin. It is in September and October that every town and village in the south of England is enlivened by their numbers and the pathetic beauty of their song; a song which I have observed as being of finer quality in England than on the continent, very possibly owing to a greater abundance of rich food. I have been even tempted to fancy that our English Robin is a finer and stouter bird than his continental relations. Certainly he is more numerous here at all times of the year, and he may travel where he pleases without fear of persecution; while the French and German Robins, who for the most part make for Italy in the autumn, return in spring in greatly diminished numbers owing to the incurable passion of the Italians for 'robins on toast.'

It does not seem that they come to us in great numbers from foreign shores, as do many others of our common birds at this time of the year; but they move northwards and southwards within our island, presumably seeking always a moderately warm climate. At Parsons' Pleasure I have seen the bushes literally alive with them in October and November, in a state of extreme liveliness and pugnacity. This is the great season of their battles. Most country-people know of the war-fare between the old and young Robins, and will generally tell you that the young ones kill their parents. The truth seems to be that after their autumnal moult, in the confidence of renewed strength, the old ones attack their offspring, and succeed in forcing them to seek new homes. This combativeness is of course accompanied by fresh vigour of song. Birds will sing, as I am pretty well convinced, under *any* kind of pleasant or exciting emotion – such as love, abundance of food, warmth, or anger; and the outbreak of the Robin's song in autumn is to be ascribed, in part at least, to the last of these. Other reasons may be found, such as restored health after the moult, or the arrival in a warmer climate after immigration, or possibly even the delusion, already noticed, which not uncommonly possesses them in a warm autumn, that it is their duty to set about pairing and nest-building already. But all these would affect other species also, and the only reason which seems to suit the idiosyncrasies of the Robin is this curious rivalry between young and old.

The Robins, I need not say, are everywhere; but there are certain kinds of birds for which we must look out in particular places. I mentioned Parsons' Pleasure just now; and we may take it very well as a starting-point, offering as it does, in a space of less than a hundred yards square, every kind of supply that a bird can possibly want; water, sedge, reeds, meadows, gravel, railings, hedges, and trees and bushes of many kinds forming abundant cover. In this cover, as you walk along the footpath towards the weir, you will very likely see a pair of Bullfinches. They were here the greater part of last winter, and are occasionally seen even in college and private gardens; but very rarely in the breeding-season or the summer, when they are away in the densest woods, where their beautiful nest and eggs are not too often found. Should they be at their usual work of devouring buds, it is well worth while to stop and watch the process; at Parsons' Pleasure they can do no serious harm, and the Bullfinch's bill is not an instrument to be lightly passed over. It places him apart from all other common English birds, and brings him into the same sub-family as the Crossbill and the Pine-Grosbeak. It is short, wide, round, and parrot-like in having the upper mandible curved downwards over the lower one, and altogether admirably suited for snipping off and retaining those fat young juicy buds.

Parsons' Pleasure stands at the narrow apex of a large island which is formed by the river Cherwell – itself here running in two channels which enclose the walk known as Mesopotamia – and the slow and often shallow stream by which Holywell mill is worked. The bird-lover will never cross the rustic bridge which brings him into the island over this latter stream, without casting a rapid glance to right and left. Here in the summer we used to listen to the Nightingale, or watch the Redstarts and Flycatchers in the willows, or feast our eyes with the splendid deep and glossy black-blue of the Swallow's back, as he darted up and down beneath the bridge in doubtful weather. And here of a winter morning you may see a pair of Moorhens paddling out of the large patch of rushes that lies opposite the bathing-place on the side of the Parks; here they breed in the summer, with only the little Reed-warblers as companions. And here there is always in winter at least a chance of seeing a Kingfisher. Why these beautiful birds are comparatively seldom to be seen in or about Oxford from March to July is a question not very easy to answer. The keeper of the bathing-place tells me that they go up to breed in ditches which run down to the Cherwell from the direction of Marston and Elsfield; and this is perhaps borne out by the discovery of a nest by a friend of mine, in a deserted quarry between Marston and Elsfield, fully a mile from the river. One would suppose, however, that the birds would be about the river, if only to supply their voracious young with food, unless we are to conclude that they feed them principally with slugs and such small-fry. Here is a point which needs investigation. The movements of the Kingfisher seem to be only partly understood, but that they do migrate, whether for short or long distances, I have no doubt whatever. On the Evenlode, another Oxfordshire river, which runs from Moreton-in-Marsh to join the Isis at Eynsham, they are rarely to be seen between March and September, or August at the earliest, while I seldom take a walk along the stream in the winter months without seeing one or more of them.

Blue is the prevailing tint of the bird as he flies from you: it is seldom that you see him coming towards you; but should that happen, the tint that you chiefly notice is the rich chestnut of the throat and breast. One Sunday morning, as I was standing on the Cherwell bank just below the Botanic

Garden, a Kingfisher, failing to see me, flew almost into my arms, shewing this chestnut hue; then suddenly wheeled, and flashed away all blue and green, towards Magdalen Bridge. I have seen a Kingfisher hovering like a dragon-fly or humming bird over a little sapling almost underneath the bridge by which you enter Addison's Walk. Possibly it was about to strike a fish but unluckily it saw me and vanished, piping shrilly. The sight was one of marvellous beauty, though it lasted but a few seconds. Can it be that the swift flash of varying liquid colour, as the bird darts from its perch into the water, is specially calculated to escape the eye of the unsuspecting minnow? It nearly always frequents streams of clear water and rather gentle flow, where its intense brightness would surely discover it, even as it sits upon a stone or bough, if its hues as seen through a liquid medium did not lose their sheen. But I must leave these questions to the philosophers, and return to Parsons' Pleasure.

The Island which I have mentioned is joined to Mesopotamia by another bridge just below the weir; and here is a second post of observation with one feature that is absent at the upper bridge. There all is silent, unless a breeze is stirring the trees; here the water prattles gently as it slides down the green slope of the weir into the deep pool below. This motion of the water makes the weir and this part of the Cherwell a favourite spot of a very beautiful little bird, which haunts it throughout the October term. All the spring and early summer the Grey Wagtail was among the noisy becks and burns of the north, bringing up his young under some spray-splashed stone, or the moist arch of a bridge; in July he comes southwards, and from that time till December or January is constantly to be seen along Cherwell and Isis. He is content with sluggish water if he can find none that is rapid; but the sound of the falling water is as surely grateful to his ear as the tiny crustaceans he finds in it are to his palate. For some time last autumn I saw him nearly every day, either on the stonework of the weir, or walking into its gentle waterslope or running lightly over the islands of dead leaves in other parts of the Cherwell; sometimes one pair would be playing among the barges on the Isis, and another at Clasper's boat-house seemed quite unconcerned at the crowd of men and boats. It is always a pleasure to watch them; and though all Wagtails have their charm for me, I give this one the first place, for its matchless delicacy of form, and the gentle grace of all its actions.

The Grey Wagtail is misnamed; it should be surely called the Long-tailed Wagtail, for its tail is nearly an inch longer than that of any other species; or the Brook-Wagtail, because it so rarely leaves the bed of the stream it haunts. All other Wagtails may be seen in meadows, ploughed fields, and uplands; but though I have repeatedly seen this one in England, Wales, Ireland, and Switzerland, I never but once saw it away from the water, and then it was for the moment upon a high road in Dorsetshire, and within a few yards of a brook and pool. Those who wish to identify it must remember its long tail and its love of water, and must also look out for the beautiful sulphur yellow of its under parts; in the spring both male and female have a black chin and throat, like our common Pied Wagtail. No picture, and no stuffed specimen, can give the least idea of what the bird is like: the specimens in our Oxford Museum look 'very sadly', as the villagers say; you must see the living bird in perpetual motion, the little feet running swiftly, the long tail ever gently flickering up and down. How can you successfully draw or stuff a bird whose most remarkable feature is never for a moment still?

While I am upon Wagtails, let me say a word for our old friend the common Pied Wagtail, who is with us in varying numbers all the year round. It is for several reasons a most interesting bird. We have known it from our childhood; but foreign bird-lovers coming to England would find it new to them, unless they chanced to come from Western France or Spain. Like one or two other species of which our island is the favourite home, it is much darker than its continental cousin the White Wagtail, when in full adult plumage. Young birds are indeed often quite a light grey, and in Magdalen cloisters and garden, where the young broods love to run and seek food on the beautifully-kept turf, almost every variety of youthful plumage may be seen in June or July, from the sombrest black to the brightest pearl-grey. Last summer, I one day spent a long time here watching the efforts of a parent to induce a young bird to leave its perch and join the others on the turf: the nest must have been placed somewhat high up among the creepers, and the young bird, on leaving it, had ventured no further than a little stone statue above my head. The mother flew repeatedly to the young one, hovered before it, chattered and encouraged it in every possible way; but it was a long time before she prevailed.

Let us now return towards the city, looking into the Parks on our way. The Curators of the Parks, not less generous to the birds than to mankind, have provided vast stores of food for the former, in the numbers of birches and conifers which flourish under their care. They, or their predecessors who stocked the plantations, seem to have had the particular object of attracting those delightful little north-country birds the Lesser Redpolls, for they have planted every kind of tree in whose seeds they find a winter subsistence. Whether they come every winter I am unable to say, and am inclined to doubt it; but in 1884, any one who went the round of the Parks, keeping an eye on the birches, could hardly fail to see them, and they have been reported not only as taking refuge here in the winter, but even as nesting in the summer.

It is one of the prettiest sights that our whole calendar of bird-life affords, to watch these tiny linnets at work in the delicate birch-boughs. They fear no human being, and can be approached within a very few yards. They almost outdo the Titmice in the amazing variety of their postures. They prefer in a general way to be upside down, and decidedly object to the common-place attitudes of more solidly built birds. Otherwise they are not remarkable for beauty at this time of year; their splendid crimson crest is hardly discernible, and the warm pink of their breasts has altogether vanished.

There are plenty of common birds to be seen even in

winter on most days in the Parks, such as the Skylark, the Yellow-hammer and its relative the Black-headed or Reed Bunting, the Pied Wagtail, the Hedge-sparrow, and others; though lawn-tennis and cricket, and new houses and brick walls, are slowly and surely driving them beyond the Cherwell for food and shelter. But there are some birds which may be seen to greater advantage in another part of Oxford, and we will take the short line to Christchurch Meadow, past Holywell Church, doubtless the abode of Owls, and the fine elms of Magdalen Park, beloved by the Woodpigeons.

All this lower part of the Cherwell, from Holywell mill to its mouth at the barges, abounds in snug and secure retreats for the birds. In Addison's Walk, as well as in the trees in Christchurch Meadow, dwell the Nuthatch and the Tree-creeper, both remarkable birds in all their ways, and each representative of a family of which no other member has ever been found in these islands. They are tree-climbing birds, but they climb in very different ways: the Creeper helping himself, like the Woodpeckers, with the downward-bent feathers of his strong tail; while the Nuthatch, having no tail to speak of, relies chiefly on his hind claw.

One is apt to think of the Creeper as a silent and very busy bird, who never finds leisure to rest and preen his feathers, or to relieve his mind with song. When he does sing he takes us a little aback. One spring morning, as I was strolling in the Broad Walk, a Creeper flew past me and fixed himself on the thick branch of an elm – not on a trunk, as usual – and uttered a loud and vigorous song, something after the manner of the Wren's. I had to turn the glass upon him to make sure that there was no mistake. This is the only occasion on which I have ever heard the Creeper sing, and it seems strange that a bird with so strong a voice should use it so seldom.

I have never but once seen the Green Woodpecker in Oxford, and that was as he flew rapidly over the Parks in the direction of the Magdalen elms. He is a much wilder bird than his near relation, the Lesser Spotted Woodpecker, who is, or was, beyond doubt an Oxford resident. I myself have not seen the bird nearer Oxford than Kennington; but I am pretty sure that it is commoner and also less shy than is generally imagined, and also that the ornitholigist who sees it is not likely to mistake it for another bird: its very small size – it is not so large as a sparrow – its crimson head, and its wings, with their black and white bars, making it a conspicuous object to a practised eye.

Christchurch Meadow is a favourite home of the Titmice. I believe that I have seen five species here within a space of a very few days: a family of Longtails, or Bottle-tits, flits from bush to bush, never associating with the others, and so justifying its scientific separation from them. Another family is to be seen in the Parks, where they build a nest every year. These delightful birds are however quite willing to live in the very centre of a town, indifferent to noise and dust. A Marsh-tit was once seen performing its antics on a lamp-post in St. Giles. A Great-tit built its nest in the stump of an old laburnum, in the little garden of Lincoln College, within a few yards of the Turl and High Street; the nest was discovered by my dog, who was prowling about the garden with a view to cats. I took great interest in this brood, which was successfully reared, and on one occasion I watched the parents bringing food to their young for twenty minutes, during which time they were fed fourteen times. The ringing note of this Great-tit or his relations is the first to be heard in that garden in winter-time, and is always welcome. The little Blue-tit is also forthcoming there at times. One Sunday morning I saw a Blue-tit climbing the walls of my College quadrangle, almost after the manner of, a Creeper, searching the crannies for insects, and even breaking down the crust of weathered stone.

But I have strayed away from Christchurch Meadow and the Botanic Garden. Here it is more especially that the Thrush tribe makes its presence felt throughout the autumn. In the Gardens the thrushes and blackbirds have become so tame from constant quiet and protection, that, they will hardly deign to move out of your way. A blackbird proceeded calmly to take his bath, in the fountain at the lower end near the meadow, one morning when I was looking on, and seemed to be fully aware of the fact that there was a locked gate between us.

Missel-thrushes are also to be seen here; and all these birds go out of a morning to breakfast on a thickly-berried thorn-bush at the Cherwell end of the Broad Walk, where they meet with their relations the Redwings, and now and then with a Fieldfare. The walker round the meadow in winter will seldom fail to hear the harsh call of the redwing, as, together with starlings innumerable, and abundance of blackbirds, they utter loud sounds of disapproval. There is one bush here whose berries must have some strange ambrosial flavour that blackbirds dearly love. All the blackbirds in Oxford seem to have their free breakfast-table here, and they have grown so bold that they will return to it again and again as I teasingly walk up and down in front of it, merely flying to a neighbouring tree when I scrutinize them too closely in search of a lingering Ring-ousel.

Rooks, Starlings, Jackdaws, and Sparrows, which abound here and everywhere else in Oxford, every one can observe for themselves, but let me remind my young readers that *every* bird is worth noticing, whether it be the rarest or the commonest. My sister laughs at me, because she once found an old copy of White's *Selborne* belonging to me, whereon was inscribed on the page devoted to the Rook, in puerile handwriting, the following annotation: 'Common about Bath' (where I was then at school). But I tell her that it was a strictly accurate scientific observation; and I only wish that I had followed it up with others equally unimpeachable.

But more out-of-the-way birds will sometimes come to Oxford, and I have seen a Kestrel trying to hover in a high wind over Christchurch Meadow, and a Heron sitting on the old gatepost in the middle of the field. Port Meadow constantly entices sea-birds when it is under water, or when the water is receding and leaving that horrible slime which is so unpleasant to the nose of man; and in fact there is hardly a wader that has not at one time or another been recorded near Oxford. Sometimes they come on migration, sometimes they are driven by stress of weather.

I have seen the bushes literally alive with them [Robins]

Oxford: Spring and Early Summer

The first balmy breath of spring brings the celandines into bloom

All the birds mentioned in the last chapter are residents in Oxford, in greater or lesser numbers according to the season, except the Fieldfares and Redwings, the Grey Wagtail, and the rarer visitors: and of these the Fieldfares and Redwings are the only true winter birds. They come from the north and east in September and October, and depart again in March and April. When we begin our Summer Term not one is to be seen. The berries in the meadow are all eaten up long before Lent Term is over, and though these are not entirely or even chiefly the Redwing's food, the birds have generally disappeared with them.

They do not however leave the country districts till later. When wild birds like these come into a town, the cause is almost certain to be stress of weather; when the winter's back is broken, they return to the fields and hedges till the approach of summer calls them northwards. There they assemble together in immense flocks, showing all the restlessness and excitement of the smaller birds that leave us in the autumn; suddenly the whole mass rises and departs like a cloud. Accounts are always forthcoming of the departure of summer migrants, and especially of the Swallows and Martins, and there are few who have not seen these as they collect on the sunny side of the house-roof, or bead the parapet of the Radcliffe building, before they make up their minds to the journey. But few have seen the Fieldfares and Redwings under the same conditions. However, on 19th March, 1884, I was lucky enough to see something of their farewell ceremonies. I was walking in some of the water-meadows adjoining a wood, on the outskirts of which were a number of tall elms and poplars, when I heard an extraordinary noise, loud, harsh, and continuous, and of great volume, proceeding from the direction of these trees, which were at the time nearly half-a-mile distant. I had been hearing the noise for a minute or two without attending to it, and was gradually developing a consciousness that some strange new agricultural instrument, or several of them, were at work somewhere near, when some Fieldfares flew past me to alight on the meadow not far off. Then putting up my glass, I saw that the trees were literally *black* with birds; and as long as I stayed, they continued there, only retreating a little as I approached, and sending foraging detachments into the meadow, or changing trees in continual fits of restlessness. The noise they made was like the deep organ-sounds of sea-birds in the breeding-time, but harsher and less serious. I would willingly have stayed to see them depart, but not knowing when that might be, I was obliged to go home: and the next day when I went to look for them, only a few were left.

These birds do not leave us as a rule before the first summer visitors have arrived. In the case I have just mentioned, the spring was a warm one, and the very next day I saw the ever-welcome Chiff-chaff, which is the earliest to come and the latest to go, of all the delicate warblers which come to find a summer's shelter in our abundant trees and herbage.

When the first balmy breath of spring brings the celandines into bloom on the hedge-bank, and when the sweet violets and primroses are beginning to feel the warmth of the sun, you may always look out for the Chiff-chaff on the sheltered side of a wood or coppice. As a rule, I see them before I hear them; if they come with an east wind, they doubtless feel chill for a day or two, or miss the plentiful supply of food which is absolutely necessary to a bird in full song. Thus in 1884, I noted 20th March as the first day on which I saw the Chiff-chaff, and 23rd March as the first on which I heard him. The next year, the month of March being less genial, I looked and listened in vain till the 31st. On that day I made a circuit round a wood to its sunny side, sheltered well from east and north, and entering for a little way one of these grassy 'rides' which are the delight of all wood-haunting birds, I stood quite still and listened. First a Robin, then a Chaffinch broke the silence; a Wood-pigeon broke away through the boughs; but no Chiff-chaff. After a while I was just turning away, when a very faint sound caught my ear, which I knew I had not heard for many months. I listened still more keenly, and caught it again; it was the prelude, the preliminary whisper, with which I have noticed that this bird, in common with a few others, is wont to work up his facilities to the effort of an outburst of song. In another minute that song was resounding through the wood.

No one who hails the approach of spring as the real beginning of a new life for men and plants and animals, can fail to be grateful to this little brown bird for putting on it the stamp and sanction of his clear resonant voice. We may grow tired of his two notes – he never gets beyond two – for he sings almost the whole summer through, and was in full voice on the 25th of September in the same year in which he began on March 23rd; but not even the first twitter of the Swallow, or the earliest song of the Nightingale, has the same hopeful story to tell me as this delicate traveller who dares the east wind and the frost. They spend the greater part of the year with us; I have seen them still lurking in sheltered corners of the Dorsetshire coast, at the beginning of October, within sound of the seawaves in which many of them must doubtless perish before they reach their journey's end.

The Willow-warbler follows his cousin to England in a very few days, and remains his companion in the trees all through the summer. He has the same brownish-yellow back and yellowish-white breast, but is a very little larger, and sings a very different song, which is unique among all British birds. Beginning with a high and tolerably full note, he drops it both in force and pitch in a cadence short and sweet, as though he were getting exhausted with the effort; for that it *is* a real effort to him and all his slim and tender relations, no one who watches as well as listens can have a reasonable doubt. This cadence is often perfect, by which I mean that it descends gradually, not of course on the notes of our musical scale, by which no birds in their natural state would deign to be fettered, but through fractions of one or perhaps two of our tones, and without returning upwards at the end; but still more often, and especially, as I fancy, after they have been here a few weeks, they take to finishing with a note nearly as high in pitch as that with which they began. This singular song is heard in summer term in every part of the Parks, and in the grass beneath the trees there must be many nests; but these we are not likely to find except by accident, so beautifully are they concealed by their grassy roofs. Through the hole in the upper part of the side you see tiny eggs, speckled with reddish brown, lying on a warm bedding of soft feathers. Though from being on the ground they probably escape the notice of Magpies and Jackdaws and other egg-devouring birds, these eggs and the young that follow must often fall a prey to stoats and weasels, rats and hedgehogs. That such creatures are not entirely absent from the neighbourhood of the Parks, I can myself bear witness, having seen one morning two fine stoats in deadly combat for some object of prey which I could not discern, as I was divided from them by the river. The piping squeaks they uttered were so vehement and loud, that at the first moment I mistook them for the alarm note of some bird that was strange to me.

One word more before we leave the Tree-warblers. In front of my drawing-room window in the country are always two rows of hedges of sweet peas, and another of edible peas; towards the end of the summer some little pale *yellow* birds come frequently and climb up and down the pea-sticks, apparently in search of insects rather than of the peas. These are the young Willow-warblers, which after their first moult assume this gently-toned yellow tint; and very graceful and beautiful creatures they are. I have sometimes seen them hover, like humming birds, over a spray on which they could not get an easy footing, and give the stem or leaves a series of rapid pecks.

Most people know the Blackcap's song who have ever lived in the country, for you can hardly enter a wood in the summer without being struck by it; and all I need do here is to distinguish it as well as I can from that of the Garden-warbler, which may easily be mistaken for it by an unpractised ear, when the birds are keeping out of sight in the foliage, as they often most provokingly will do. Both are essentially warblers; that is, they sing a *strain* of music, continuous and *legato*, instead of a song that is broken up into separate notes or short phrases, like that of the Song-thrush, or the Chiff-chaff. But they differ in two points: the strain of the Blackcap is shorter, forming in fact one lengthened phrase 'in sweetness long drawn out', while the Garden-warbler will go on almost continuously for many minutes together: and secondly, the Blackcap's music is played upon a mellower instrument. The most gifted Blackcaps – for birds of the same species differ considerably in their power of song – excel all other birds in the soft *quality* of their tone. So far as I have been able to observe, the Blackcap's voice is almost entirely wanting in that power of producing the harmonics of a note which gives a musical sound its brilliant quality; but this very want is what produces its unrivalled mellowness.

Oxford: Spring and Early Summer

Two other members of this group of warblers are the two Whitethroats, greater and lesser, and we have not far to go to find them. They arrive just at the beginning of our Easter Term, but never come to Oxford in great numbers, because their proper homes, the hedgerows, are naturally not common objects of a town. In the country the greater Whitethroats are swarming this year (1885), and in most years they are the most abundant of our eight warblers; and the smaller bird, less seen and less showy, makes his presence felt in almost every lane and meadow by the brilliancy of his note.

Where shall we find a hedge near at hand, where we may learn to distinguish the two birds? We left the Blackcaps and Garden-warblers at the upper end of the Park; we shall still have a chance of listening to them if we take the walk towards Parsons' Pleasure, and here in the thorn-hedge on the right hand of the path, we shall find both the Whitethroats. As we walk along, a rough grating sound, something like the noise of a diminutive corn-crake, is heard on the other side of the hedge – stopping when we stop, and sounding ahead of us as we walk on. This is the teasing way of the greater Whitethroat, and it means that he is either building a nest in the hedge, or thinking of doing so. If you give him time, however, he will show himself, flirting up to the top of the hedge, crooning, craking, and popping into it again; then flying out a little way, cheerily singing a soft and truly warbling song, with fluttering wings and roughened feathers, and then perhaps perching on a twig to repeat it. Now you see the white of his throat; it is real white, and it does not go below the throat. In fact the throat of both Whitethroats is real white, and they have a pleasant way of puffing it out, as if to assure one that there is no mistake about it.

But how to distinguish the two? for in size they differ hardly enough to guide an inexperienced eye. There are three points of marked difference. The larger bird has a rufous or rusty-coloured back, and his wing-coverts are of much the same colour; while the back of the lesser bird is

47

darkish or greyish brown. Secondly, the head of the lesser Whitethroat is of a much darker bluish-grey tint. But much the best point of distinction in the breeding season is in the song. As I have said, the larger bird warbles; but the lesser one, after a little preliminary soliloquy in an under-tone, bursts out into a succession of high notes, all of exactly the same pitch. It took me some time to find out who was the performer of this music which I heard so constantly in the hedges, for the bird is very restless and very modest. When I caught sight of him he would not stop to be examined closely. One day however he was kind enough to alight for a moment in a poplar close by me, and as I watched him in the loosely-leaved branches, he poured out the song, and duly got the credit for it.

We are now close to our old winter-station on the bridge over the mill-stream, and leaning over it once more on the upper side, we shall hear, if not see, both the remaining species of the warblers that Oxford has to show us. They are the only species of River-warblers that are *known* to visit England regularly every year; these two, the Sedge-warbler and the Reed-warbler, never fail, and the Sedge-warbler comes in very large numbers.

Why should the Reed-warbler be so much less generally distributed than the Sedge-warbler? That it is so, we can show well enough even from Oxford alone. You will find Sedge-warblers all along the Cherwell and the Isis, wherever there is a bit of cover, and very often they will turn up where least expected; in a corn-field, for example, where I have seen them running up and down the corn-stalks as if they were their native reeds. But you must either know where to find the Reed-warbler, or learn by slow degrees.

There is, however, at least a plausible answer to the question. Owing to the prime necessity of *reeds* for the building of this deep-sheltered nest, which is swung between several of them, kept firm by their centrifugal tendency, yielding lovingly yet proudly to every blast of wind or current of water – owing to this necessity, the Reed-warbler declines to take up his abode in any place where the reeds are not thick enough and tall enough to give a real protection to himself and his brood. Now in the whole length of Isis between Kennington and Godstow, and of Cherwell between its mouth and Parsons' Pleasure, there is no reed-bed which answers all the requirements of this little bird. Now and then, it is true, they will leave the reeds for some other nesting-place; one of them sang away all the Summer Term of 1884 in the bushes behind the Museum, nearly half a mile from the river, and probably built a nest among the lilac-bushes which there abound. But that year they seemed to be more abundant than usual; and this, perhaps, was one for whom there was no room in the limited space of the reeds at Parsons' Pleasure. Thick bushes, where many lithe saplings spring from a common root, would suit him better than a scanty reed-bed.

There is no great difficulty in distinguishing Sedge- and Reed-warblers, if you have an eye for the *character* of birds. The two are very different in temperament, though both are of the same quiet brown, with whitish breast. The Sedge-bird is a restless, noisy, impudent little creature, not at all modest or retiring, and much given to mocking the voices of other birds. This is done as a rule in the middle of one of his long and continuous outpourings of chatter; but I one day heard a much more ridiculous display of impertinence. I was standing at the bottom of the Parks, looking at a pair or two of Sedge-warblers on a bush, and wondering whether they were going to build a nest there, when a Blackbird emerged from the thicket behind me, and seeing a human being, set up that absurd cackle that we all know so well. Instantly, out of the bush I was looking at, there came an echo of this cackle, uttered by a small voice in such ludicrous tones of mockery, as fairly to upset my gravity. It seemed to say, 'You awkward idiot of a bird, I can make that noise as well as you: only listen!' –

The Reed-warbler, on the other hand, is quieter and gentler, and utters, by way of song, a long crooning soliloquy, in accents not sweet, but much less harsh and declamatory than those of his cousin. I have listened to him for half-an-hour together among the bushes that border the reed-bed, and have fancied that his warble suits well with the gentle flow of the water, and the low hum of the insects around me. He will sit for a long time singing on the same twig, while his partner is on her nest in the reeds below; but the Sedge-warbler, in this and other respects like a fidgety and ill-trained child, is never in one place, or in the same vein of song, for more than a minute at a time.

It is amusing to stand and listen to the two voices going on at the same time; the Sedge-bird rattling along in a state of the intensest excitement, pitching up his voice into a series of loud squeaks, and then dropping it into a long-drawn grating noise, like the winding-up of an old-fashioned watch, while the Reed-warbler, unaffected by all this volubility, takes his own line in a continued prattle of gentle content and self-sufficiency.

These eight birds, then, are the *warblers* which at present visit Oxford. Longer walks and careful observation may no doubt bring us across at least two others, the Wood-warbler and the Grasshopper-warbler: the nest of the Wood-warbler has been found within three miles. Another bird, too, which is often called a warbler, has of late become very common both in and about Oxford – the Redstart. Four or five years ago they were getting quite rare; but this year (1885) the flicker of the red tail is to be seen all along the Cherwell, in the Broad Walk, where they build in holes of the elms, in Port Meadow, where I have heard the gentle warbling song from the telegraph wires, and doubtless in most gardens. The Redstart is so extremely beautiful in summer, his song so tender and sweet, and all his ways so gentle and trustful, that if he were as common, and stayed with us all the year, he would certainly put our Robin's popularity to the proof. Nesting in our garden, or even on the very wall of our house, and making his presence there obvious by his brilliant colouring and his fearless domesticity, he might become, like his plainer cousin of the continent, the favourite of the peasant, who looks to his arrival in spring as the sign of a better time approaching.

The Oxford Redstarts find convenient holes for their nests in the pollard willows which line the banks of the Cherwell and the many arms of the Isis. The same unvaried and unnatural form of tree, which looks so dreary and ghastly in the waste of winter flood, is full of comfort and adaptability for the bird in summer. The works of man, though not

The flicker of a red tail is to be seen all along the Cherwell

always beautiful, are almost always turned to account by the birds, and by many kinds preferred to the solitude of wilder haunts. Whether he builds houses, or constructs railways, or digs ditches, or forces trees into an unnatural shape, they are ready to take advantage of every chance he gives them. Only when the air is poisoned by smoke and drainage, and vegetation retreats before the approach of slums, do they leave their natural friends to live without the charm of their voices – all but that strange parasite of mankind, the Sparrow. He, growing sootier every year, and doing his useful dirty work with untiring diligence and appetite, lives on his noisy and quarrelsome life even in the very heart of London.

Whether the surroundings of the Oxford Sparrows have given them a sense of higher things, I cannot say; but they have ways which have suggested to me that the Sparrow must at some period of his existence have fallen from a higher state. No sooner does the summer begin to bring out the flies among our pollard willows, than they become alive with Sparrows. There you may see them, as you repose on one of the comfortable seats on the brink of the Cherwell in the Parks, catching flies in the air with a vigour and address which in the course of a few hundred years might almost develop into elegance. Again and again I have had to turn my glass upon a bird to see if it could really be a Sparrow that was fluttering in the air over the water with an activity apparently meant to rival that of the little Fly-catcher, who sits on a bough at hand, and occasionally performs the same feat with native lightness and deftness. But these are for the most part young Sparrows of the year, who have been brought here perhaps by their parents to be out of the way of cats, and for the benefit of country air and an easily-digested insect diet. How long they stay here I do not know; but before our Autumn Term begins they must have migrated back to the city, for I seldom or never see them in the willows except in the Summer Term.

These seats by the Cherwell are excellent stations for observation. Swallows, Martins, and Sand-martins flit over the water; Swifts scream overhead towards evening; Greenfinches trill gently in the trees, or utter that curious lengthened sound which is something between the bleat of a lamb and the snore of a light sleeper; the Yellow Wagtail, lately arrived, walks before you on the path, looking for materials for a nest near the water's edge; the Fly-catcher, latest arrival of all, is perched in silence on the railing, darting now and then into the air for flies; the Corn-crake sounds from his security beyond the Cherwell, and a solitary Nightingale, soon to be driven away by dogs and boats and bathers, may startle you with a burst of song from the neighbouring thicket.

Of the birds just mentioned, the Swifts, Swallows, and

Martins build, I need hardly say, in human habitations, the Sand-martins in some sand or gravel-pit, occasionally far away from the river. The largest colony of these little brown birds, so characteristic of our Oxford summer, is in a large sand-pit on Foxcombe Hill: there, last July, I chanced to see the fledglings peeping out of their holes into the wide world, like children gazing from a nursery window. The destruction all these species cause among the flies which swarm round Oxford must be enormous. One day a Martin dropped a cargo of flies out of its mouth on to my hat, just as it was about to be distributed to the nestlings; a magnifying glass revealed a countless mass of tiny insects, some still alive and struggling. One little wasp-like creature disengaged himself from the rest, and crawled down my hand, escaping literally from the very jaws of death.

Before I leave these birds of summer, let me record the fact that last June (1886) a pair of swallows built their nest on the circular spring of a bell just over a doorway behind the University Museum; the bell was constantly being rung, and the nest was not unfrequently examined, but they brought up their young successfully. This should be reassuring to those who believe that the Museum and its authorities are a terror to living animals.

A Midland Village:
Garden and Meadow

Seasons when storms are especially frequent and violent

The traveller by railway from Oxford to Worcester leaves the broad meadows of the Isis about three miles above Oxford, and after crossing a spur of higher land, strikes the little river Evenlode at Handborough Station, not far from its junction with the Isis at Cassington. This Evenlode is the next considerable stream westward of the Cherwell, and just as the line of the latter is followed by the Birmingham railway, so the line to Worcester keeps closely to the Evenlode for nearly twenty miles, only leaving it at last in its cradle in the uplands of Worcestershire. Westward again of the Evenlode, the Windrush comes down from the northern Cotswolds, to join the Isis at Witney, and further still come

Leach and Coln, and others, bringing the clear cold water in which trout delight, from the abundant springs at North-leach and Andoversford. But the Evenlode is not a Cotswold stream, though trout may still be caught in it where it has not been polluted; it skirts for many miles the north-eastern slope of the Cotswolds, which may be seen from the train-windows closing in the horizon all the way from Shipton-under-Wychwood to Evesham and Worcester, but it has the slow current and muddy bottom of a lowland stream, and runs throughout its course among water-meadows liable to flood.

For the first few miles of its course it is little more than a ditch; but shortly after passing the historic lawns of Daylesford, it is joined by two other streams, one descending from the slope of the Cotswolds, and the other from the high ground of Chipping Norton eastwards. These two join the Evenlode exactly at the point where it enters Oxfordshire, and the combination produces a little river of some preten-sion, which enjoys a somewhat more rapid descent for some miles from this junction, and almost prattles as it passes the ancient abbey-lands of Bruern and the picturesque spire of Shipton church.

Close to the point of junction, on a long tongue of land which is a spur of Daylesford hill, and forms a kind of promontory bounded by the meadows of the Evenlode and the easternmost of its two tributaries, lies the village where much of my time is spent in vacations. It is more than four hundred feet above the sea, and the hills around it rise to double that height; but it lies in an open country, abounding in corn, amply provided with hay-meadows by the alluvial deposit of the streams already mentioned, and also within easy reach of long stretches of wild woodland. For all along the valley the observant passenger will have been struck with the long lines of wood which flank the Evenlode at intervals throughout its course; he passes beneath what remains of the ancient forest of Wychwood, and again after a considerable gap he has the abbey-woods of Bruern on his left, and once more after an interval of cultivation his view is

shut in by the dense fox-covers of Bledington and Oddington, the border villages of Gloucestershire. It is just at this
interval between Bruern and Bledington that the junction of
the two streams with the Evenlode takes place; so that from
this point, or from the village already spoken of, it is but a
short distance to an ample and solitary woodland either up
or down the valley. Beyond that woodland lies a stretch of
pasture land which brings you to the foot of the long ridge of
hill forming the north-eastern boundary and bulwark of the
Cotswolds, and hiding from us the little old-world towns of
Burford and Northleach. We have therefore within a radius
of five or six miles almost every kind of country in which
birds rejoice to live. We have water-meadow, cornland,
woods, and hills, and also here and there a few acres of
scrubby heath and gorse; and the only requisite we lack is a
large sheet of water or marshy ground, which might attract
the waders and sea-birds so commonly found near Oxford.
We are neither too far north to miss the southern birds, nor
too far south to see the northern ones occasionally; we might
with advantage be a little farther east, but we are not too far
west to miss the Nightingale from our coverts.

Such a position and variety would be sure to produce a
long list of birds, both residents and visitors; not only
because there are localities at hand suited to be their
dwelling-places during the whole or part of the year, but
because they offer the *change of scene and food* which is essential
to the welfare of many species. An open country of heath and
common will not abound in birds of more than a very few
species, unless it is varied with fertile oases, with garden,
orchard, or meadow; for many of the birds that delight to
play about in the open, and rove from place to place during
the first few months of their existence, will need for their
nests and young the shelter of trees and shrubs. While the
young are growing, they require incessant feeding, and the
food must be at hand which they can best assimilate and
digest; and it does not follow that this is the same as that
which the parents habitually eat, or which the young themselves will most profit by when they are fledged.

But to return to my village; it is astonishing how many birds, in spite of the presence of their deadliest enemies, boys and cats, will come into our gardens to build their nests, if only fair opportunities are offered them. In a garden close to my own, whose owner has used every means in his power to attract them, there were last May fifty-three nests, exclusive of those of swallows and martins. The garden is not more than two or three acres in extent, including the little orchard which adjoins it; but by planting great numbers of thick bushes and coniferous trees, and by placing flower-pots, old wooden boxes, and other such odds and ends, in the forks of the branches at a considerable height from the ground, he has inspired them with perfect confidence in his goodwill and 'philornithic' intentions. The fact that a pair of Missel-thrushes reared their young here only a few feet from the ground, and close to a stable and a much-frequented walk, shows that even birds of wild habits of life may be brought to repose trust in man by attention to their wants and wishes. The Blackcap, which almost always nests in woods, had here found it possible to take up its quarters close to the fruit it loves; and of all the commoner kinds the nests were legion. Three Greenfinches built in the same tree one over another, the nests being little more than a foot apart; a Wren had so closely fitted a little box with the usual materials of its nest, that the door corresponded with the only opening in the box; a Robin had found an ample basis of construction in the deserted nest of a Blackbird. The only bird that had been forbidden access to this Eden was the Bullfinch; he duly made his appearance, but was judged to be too dangerous to the buds of the fruit-trees. Siskins and Hawfinches have occasionally looked into this garden; but the Hawfinch has never bred here, and for some unexplained reason the same is the case with the Redstart.

In my own garden, within a few feet of the house, this last-mentioned friend found a very convenient abode in a hole in my largest apple tree. The parents became very tame, and when they knew their young were discovered, made very little scruple about exposing themselves in going in and out.

The food they brought their young, whenever we happened to see it, was a small green caterpillar; and I sincerely hope we may have them again next year, both for the benefit to my garden and for the pleasure they give me. May the sad loss of one fledgling depart from their memory before next summer! It was just launched into the world when it fell a victim to my dog, for I had seen it in the nest only an hour or two before; I had left strict injunctions for the confinement of all domestic animals as soon as the young were seen to leave the nest, but had not expected them to face the world so soon. This was a beautiful little bird, showing already the rich russet colour in what he had of tail; his legs and claws were of extreme slightness and delicacy, and his whole colouring and frame-work was far more engaging than is the case with most young birds of his age. He had already picked up, or had been given by his mother, a pebble or two to assist his digestion.

The Redstart was not a very common bird about us until about three years ago, but now its gentle song is heard in May in almost every garden and well-hedged field. In August and September the young birds are everywhere seen showing their conspicuous fire-tails as they flit in and out of the already fast-browning hedges; yet three or four years ago my daily walks did not discover more than a few dozen in a summer. What can be the cause of this surprising increase of population? If it is anything that has happened in this country, such as the passing of the Wild Birds' Protection Act, we must suppose that the same individuals which breed and are born here in one spring, return here the next year; i.e. our supply of this summer migrant depends on the treatment it receives here, and not upon the number of Redstarts available in the world generally. I am inclined indeed to think, though it is difficult to prove it, that the wholesale slaughter of young birds in our neighbourhood is less horrible than it used to be before the passing of the Act; but when we remember that other creatures, certain butter-flies, for example, whose relations to man never greatly differ from year to year, are found to be much more abundant in some years than others, the more rational conclusion seems to be, that an increase or decrease of numbers depends, in the case of *migrating birds*, on certain causes which are beyond the reach of mankind to regulate. What these may be it is possible only to guess. A famine in the winter quarters would rapidly decimate the numbers of those individuals which were with us last summer, and we cannot tell whether the deficiency would be supplied from other sources. Even a severe storm in the spring or autumn journey would destroy an immense number of birds so tender and fragile; and we must not forget that these journeys take place at the very seasons when storms are especially frequent and violent. Any very serious alteration in the methods of dealing with the land in this country, such as the substitution of railings or ditches for hedges, or the wholesale felling of woods and copses, would also most certainly affect the numbers of this and most other birds; but in the course of the last few years no such change of any magnitude has taken place, and the increase of the Redstarts must be put down, I think, to causes taking effect beyond the sea.

The only really annoying destruction of hedges in our immediate neighbourhood within my recollection is one for which I ought always to be grateful, for it brought me a sight of the only Black Redstart I have ever seen in England. On the 6th November, 1884, I was returning from a morning walk, and about a mile from the village came to a spot which a few years ago was one of the prettiest in the countryside. Here one road crosses another, and formerly the crossing was enclosed by high hedges and banks, forming a comfortable nook where the Sand-martins bored their way into the light and sandy soil. A land-agent descended here one day like a bird of ill omen, and swept the hedges away, filling their place with long lines of bare and ugly wall; the martins sought a lodging elsewhere, for they could no longer feed their young with the insect-life of the hedgerows; and my associations with the spot were broken. But it was upon this very wall, new, useful, straight, and intensely human, that this rare little bird chose to sun himself that bright November morning. A thousand times have I seen him on the old grey fern-covered walls of the Alpine passes, but never did I expect to see him on this hideous 'improvement' of civilization. Except that he was silent and alone, he seemed as much at home here as on the flowery slopes of the Engstlen-alp. There is nothing that man can erect that is too uncomely for the birds.

I have digressed for a moment to tell this tale of the Black Redstart, but I have hardly yet done with the village itself. We have of course plenty of Robins and Hedge-sparrows breeding in our gardens, and in the nests of these the Cuckoo is fond of depositing its egg. It would not be always true to say that the Cuckoo *lays* its egg in its victim's nest for in some instances at least the egg is dropped from the bill. A Robin built its nest in a hole in the wall of my garden, several inches deep, and with a rather narrow entrance; several eggs were laid and all was going well. It was three or four days from my first knowledge of the nest to my second visit, when I was greatly annoyed to find all the eggs but one on the ground at the foot of the wall, broken to fragments. I accused the boy who filled the office of boot-cleaner; he was more or less of a pickle, but he positively denied all complicity. Meanwhile in my indignation I had forgotten to examine the remaining egg; but the mystery was soon solved. Noticing that the Robins had not deserted, I looked again after a while, and found a young Cuckoo. The ugly wretch grew rapidly, and soon became too big for the nest, so we hung him up in a basket on a branch, where the Robins continued to feed him. His aspect and temper were those of a young fiend. If you looked at him he would swell with passion, and if you put your finger towards him, he would rise up in the basket and 'go for it'. One fine morning he disappeared, and was never heard of more.

In this case the egg was unquestionably deposited with the bill, while the same instrument must have been used to eject the Robin's eggs, thus saving the young Cuckoo when hatched the trouble of getting rid of the young Robins by muscular exertions. Next year a Cuckoo's egg was laid in a Hedge-sparrow's nest in an adjoining garden; but the intended foster-parents wisely deserted, and I was able to take possession of the nest and eggs. Every year in June we are sure to notice a persistent cuckooing close by us, and nearly every year an egg is found in some nest in the village. Once (I think it was at the time when the Robin was the victim) boys reported that they saw a cuckoo sitting on a bough hard by, *with an egg in its bill.* There is no doubt whatever that the bill can hold the egg, which is hardly as large as a starling's!

We have another smaller bird in the village which can hold large objects between its mandibles – objects almost as large, and sometimes more bulky, than the egg of the Cuckoo. This is the Nuthatch, which will carry away from a window any number of hard dessert nuts, and store them up in all sorts of holes and corners, where they are sometimes found still unbroken. These plump and neat little birds, whose bills and heads and necks seem all of a piece, while their bodies and tails are not of much account, have been for years accustomed to come for their dinners to my neighbour's windows. One day while sitting with my friend, Col. Barrow, we set the Nuthatches a task which at first puzzled them. After letting them carry off a number of nuts in the usual way, we put the nuts into a glass tumbler. The birds arrived, they saw the nuts, and tried to get at them, but in vain. Some invisible obstacle was in the way; they must have thought it most uncanny. They poked and prodded, and eventually departed. Again they came, and a third time, with the like result. At last one of them took his station on a bit of wood erected for perching purposes just over the lintel; he saw the nuts below him, down he came upon the tumbler's edge, and in a moment his long neck was stretched downwards and the prize won. The muscular power of the bird is as well shown by this feat, as his perseverance and sagacity by the discovery of the trick; for holding on by his prehensile claws to the edge of the tumbler, he contrived to seize with his bill a large nut placed in the bottom of it, without any assistance from his wings; the length of the tumbler being little less than that of the bird. But after all, this was no more than a momentary use of the same posture in which he is often to be seen, as he runs down the trunks of trees in search of insects.

The Spotted Flycatcher is another little bird which abounds in our gardens and orchards; it is always pleasant to watch, and its nest is easy to find. One pair had the audacity to build on the wall of the village school: it was much as if a human being should take up his residence in a tiger's jungle, but if I recollect right, the eggs and young escaped harm. Another pair placed their nest on a sun-dial in Col. Barrow's garden, as late as mid-July. This Flycatcher is the latest of all the summer migrants to arrive on our shores; the males and females seem to come together, and begin the work of nesting at once, i.e. in the middle of May; if the nest is taken as was probably the case with this pair, the second brood would not be hatched till July. The bird is singularly silent, never getting (within my experience) beyond an oft-repeated and half-whispered phrase, which consist of three notes, or rather sounds, and no more; the first is higher and louder than the others, which are to my mind much like that curious sound of disappointment or anxiety which we produce by applying the tongue to the roof of the mouth, and then suddenly withdrawing it. But is the Flycatcher always and everywhere a silent bird? It is most singular that he should be unattractive in colour also – grey and brown and insignificant; but perhaps in the eyes of his wife even his quiet voice and grey figure may have weight.

The Flycatcher is an excellent study for a young ornithologist. He is easily seen, perching almost always on a leafless bough or railing, whence he may have a clear view, and be able to pick and choose his flies; and he will let you come quite close, without losing his presence of mind. His attitude is so unique, that I can distinguish his tiny form at the whole length of the orchard; he sits quietly, silently, the tail slightly drooped and still, the head, with longish narrow bill, bent a little downwards, for his prey is almost always below him; suddenly this expectant repose is changed into quick and airy action, the little wings hover here and there so quickly that you cannot follow them, the fly is caught, and he returns with it in his bill to his perch, to await a safe moment for carrying it to its young. All this is done so unobtrusively by a little greyish-brown bird with greyish-white breast, that hundreds of his human neighbours never know of his existence in their gardens. He is wholly unlike his handsomer and livelier namesake, the Pied Flycatcher, in all those outward characteristics which attract the inexperienced eye; but the essential features are alike in both, the long wing, the bill flat at the base, and the gape of the mouth furnished with strong hairs, which act like the backward-bent teeth of the pike in preventing the escape of the prey.

Our village is so placed, that all the birds that nest in our gardens and orchards have easy and immediate access to a variety of feeding-grounds. From my window, I look over the village allotments, where all kinds of birds can be supplied with what they need, whether they be grain-eating or grub-eating; here come the Rooks, from the rookery close by, and quite unconscious of my presence behind the window, and regardless of the carcases of former comrades which swing on some of the allotments, they turn out the grubs with those featherless white bills which are still as great a mystery as the serrated claw of the Nightjar.

Here also come the Wood-pigeons, and in late summer the Turtle-doves – far worse enemies to the cottager than the rooks; here all the common herd of Blackbirds, Thrushes, Sparrows, Chaffinches, and Greenfinches, help to clear the growing vegetables of crawling pests at the rate of hundreds and thousands a day, yet the owners of the allotments have been accustomed since their childhood to destroy every winged thing that comes within their cruel reach.

Short-sighted, unobservant as they are, they decline to be instructed on matters of which they know very little, but stick to what they know like limpets. For my part, I decline to protect my gooseberries and currants from the birds; their ravages are grossly exaggerated, and what they get I do not grudge them, considering their services during the rest of the year.

Beyond the allotments the ground falls to the brook which I mentioned as descending from Chipping Norton to join the Evenlode. This brook is dammed up just below to supply an old flour-mill, and has been so used for centuries; its bed is therefore well lined with mud, and when the water is let out, which often happens, this mud appears in little banks under the shelving rat-riddled lip of the meadow. Here is a chance for some of the more unusual birds, as every ornithologist would say if he saw the stream; but both water and mud are often thick with the dye from the Chipping Norton tweed-mill and no trout will live below the point at which the poisoned water comes in. Strange to say, the poisoning does not seem to affect the birds. Two pairs of Grey Wagtails, which I seldom see in the Evenlode, passed a happy time here from July to December last year, preferring some turn of the brook where the water broke over a few stones or a miniature weir; and through August and September they were joined by several Green Sandpipers. These beautiful birds, whose departure I always regret, are on their way from their breeding-places in the North to some winter residence; they stay only a few weeks in England, and little is known about them. Many a time have I stalked them, looking far along the stream with a powerful glass in hopes of catching them at work with their long bills; each effort comes to the same provoking conclusion, the bird suddenly shooting up from beneath your feet, just at a place which you fancied you had most carefully scanned. When they first arrive they will fly only to a short distance, and the bright white of their upper tail-feathers enables you to mark them down easily for a second attempt; but after a few days they will rise high in the air, like a snipe, when disturbed, and uttering their shrill pipe, circle round and round, and finally vanish.

It should be noted that this species is called the *Green* Sandpiper because its legs are green; such are the wilful ways of English terminology. It is the only Sandpiper we have, beside the common species, which invariably prefers the Evenlode, where it may every now and then be seen working its rapid way along the edge of the water quite unconcerned at a spectator, and declining to go off like a champagne cork. Both kinds come in spring and late summer, but the Green Sandpiper is much more regular in his visits, and stays with us, in autumn at least, much longer. A stray pair found their way here last winter in a hard frost, and rose from beneath my feet as I walked along the Evenlode on 24th December. This is the only time I have ever seen them here except in the other brook; and I have very little doubt that they were total strangers to the locality. Had they ever been here before, I make bold to say that they would have gone to their old haunts.

Beyond the brook lies a magnificent meadow nearly a mile long, called the Yantle. This meadow was once doubtless the common pasture ground of the parish: it is now favoured by great numbers of winged families bred in our gardens and orchards. Goldfinches, linnets, starlings, redstarts, pipits, wagtails, whitethroats, and a dozen or two of other kinds, spend their whole day here when the broods are reared. The Yellow Wagtails are always conspicuous objects; not that they are brilliantly coloured, for the young ones are mostly brown on the back, and would hardly catch an inexperienced eye, but because of the playfulness of their ways and their graceful, wavy flight. Young birds play just like kittens, or like the fox-cubs I once caught playing in Daylesford wood at the mouth of their earth, and watched for a long time as they rolled and tumbled over each other. Only yesterday (15th July, 1885) I watched a host of young willow-wrens, whitethroats, titmice, and others, sporting with each other in a willow coppice, and mixing together without much reserve. Once I was taken aback by the sight of two young buntings at play; for a time they quite deceived me by their agility, fluttering in the air like linnets, unconscious that a single winter was to turn them into burly and melancholy buntings. The student of birds who sighs when the breeding season is over and the familiar voices are mute, is consoled by the sight of all these bright young families, happy in youth, liberty and abundance. His knowledge, too, is immensely increased by the study of their habits and appearance. His sense of the ludicrous is also sometimes touched, as mine was yesterday when I went to see how my young swallows were getting on under the roof of an outhouse, and found them all sitting in a row on a rafter, like school-children; or when the young goldfinches in the chestnut tree grew too big for their nest, but would persist in sitting in it till they sat it all out of shape, and no one could make out how they contrived to hold on by it any longer. Young birds too, like young trout, are much less suspicious than old ones, and will often let you come quite close to them. In Magdalen Walk at Oxford the young birds delight to hop about on the gravel path, supplying themselves, I suppose, with the pebbles which they need for digestion; and here one day in July a young Robin repeatedly let me come within two yards of him, at which distance from me he picked up a fat green caterpillar, swallowed it with great gusto, and literally smacked his bill afterwards. The very close examination thus afforded me of this living young Robin disclosed a strong rufous tint on the tail-coverts, of which I can find nothing in descriptions of the bird; if this is usually the case, it should indicate a close connection with the Redstarts, the young of which resemble the young Robin also in the mottled brown of the rest of their plumage.

Our meadows are liable to flood occasionally in the winter, and also in a summer wetter than usual. One stormy day in July, some years ago, I espied two common Gulls standing in the water of a slight flood, apparently quite at home. But our Rooks found them out, and considering the Yantle sacred to themselves and such small birds as they might be graciously pleased to allow there, proceeded to worry them by flying round and round above them incessantly until the poor birds were fain to depart. Rooks are very hostile to intruders, and quite capable of continued teasing; I have watched them for a whole morning persecuting a Kestrel. No sooner did the Kestrel alight on the ground than the Rooks 'went for it', and drove it away; and wherever it went they pursued it, backwards and forwards, over a space of two or three miles.

A Midland Village: Garden and Meadow

In winter the floods will sometimes freeze. One very cold day, as I was about to cross the ice-bound meadow, I saw some little things in motion at the further end, like feathers dancing about on the ice, which my glass discovered to be the tails of a family of Long-tailed Tits. They were pecking away at the ice, with their tails high in the air. As I neared them they flew away, and marking the place where they were at work, I knelt down on the ice and examined it with the greatest care. Not a trace of anything eatable was to be found. Were they trying to substitute ice for water? Not a drop of water was to be found anywhere near. I have seen Fieldfares and Redwings doing the same thing in Christ Church meadow at Oxford, but the unfrozen Cherwell was within a few yards of them. Whether or no the Long-tails were trying to appease their thirst, I may suggest to those who feed the starving birds in winter, that they should re-member that water as well as food is necessary to support life.

The Yantle is a great favourite with Plovers, Turtle-doves, and Wood-pigeons, and in the winter it is much patronized by Fieldfares and Redwings. And a day or two ago I sur-prised four Curlew here (21st March) on their way from the sea to their inland breeding places. But enough of the village and its gardens and outlying meadows; in the next chapter we will stroll further afield.

So we hung him up in a basket on a branch

A Midland Village:
Railway and Woodland

I walk alongside the railway

Beyond the Yantle we come upon a line of railway, running down from Chipping Norton to join the main line to Worcester. Just as the waters of the Evenlode are reinforced at this point in its course by the two contingent streams I described in the last chapter, so the main railway is here joined by two subsidiary lines, the one coming from Chipping Norton and the other from Cheltenham over the Cotswolds. Paradoxical as it may seem, I do not hesitate to say that this large mileage of railway within a small radius acts beneficially upon our bird-life. Let us see how this is.

In the first place, both cuttings and embankments, as soon as they are well overgrown with grass, afford secure and sunny nesting-places to a number of birds which build their nests on the ground. The Whinchat for example, an abundant bird here every summer, gives the railway-banks its especial patronage. The predatory village-boys cannot prowl about these banks with impunity except on Sundays, and even then are very apt to miss a Whinchat's nest. You may see the cock-bird sitting on the telegraph wires, singing his peaceful little song, but unless you disturb his wife from her beautiful blue eggs you are very unlikely to find them in the thickening grass of May or June. And even if she is on the nest, she will sit very close; I have seen an express train fly past without disturbing her, when the nest was but six or eight feet from the rails. The young, when reared, will often haunt the railway for the rest of the summer, undismayed by the rattle and vibration which must have shaken them even when they were still within the egg. Occasionally a Wheatear will make its appearance about the railway, but I have no evidence of its breeding there; nor is the Stonechat often to be seen here, though it is a summer visitor not far off among the hills.

Let me say incidentally that no one who has either good eyes or a good glass ought ever to confound the two Chats together. In the breeding season the fine black head of the cock Stonechat distinguishes him at once; but even the female should never be the subject of a blunder, if the observer has been at all used to attend to the *attitudes* of birds. The Stonechat sits upright and almost defiant, and is a shorter and stouter bird than the Whinchat, which perches in an attitude of greater humility, and always seems to me to deprecate your interference rather than to defy it. And it is quite in keeping with this that the 'chat' of the latter is not so loud and resonant as that of the former, as I have satisfied myself after careful observation of both; the Stonechat penetrating to my dull ears at a greater distance than his cousin. This really means that the bill of the one, and in fact his whole muscular system, is stronger than the same in the other.

If I walk alongside of the railway, as it passes between the water-meadows and the cornfields which lie above them, divided on each side from these by a low-lying withy-bed, I always keep an eye upon the telegraph wires ahead, knowing by long experience that they will tell me what birds are breeding or have bred about here. As autumn approaches, great numbers indeed of visitors, Swallows, Martins, Linnets, and others, will come and sun themselves here, and even tempt a Sparrow-hawk or Kestrel to beat up and down the line; but in early summer, beside the Whinchats, and the Whitethroats nesting in great numbers in the thick quickset hedges which border the line, it is chiefly the melancholy tribe of Buntings that will attract my notice.

I trust my friends the Buntings will not take offence at being called melancholy; I cannot retract the word, except in what is now called 'a parliamentary sense'. I have just been looking through a series of plates and descriptions of all the Buntings of Europe, and in almost every one of them I see the same deflected tail and listless attitude, and read of the same monotonous and continually repeated note. The Buntings form in fact, though apt to be confused with one another owing to their very strong family likeness, perhaps the most clearly-marked and idiosyncratic genus among the whole range of our smaller birds. This may be very easily illustrated from our three common English species. Look at the common Corn Bunting, as he sits on the wires or the hedge-top; he is lumpy, loose-feathered, spiritless, and flies off with his legs hanging down and without a trace of agility or vivacity; he is a dull bird, and seems to know it. Even his voice is half-hearted; it reminds me often of an old man in our village who used to tell us that he had 'a wheezing in his pipes'. Near him sits a Yellow Bunting (Yellowhammer), a beautiful bird when in full adult plumage of yellow head, orange-brown back, white outer tail-feathers, and pink legs; yet even this valued old friend is apt to be untidy in the sit of his feathers, to perch in a melancholy brown study with deflected tail and to utter the same old song all the spring and summer through. This song, however (if indeed it can be called one), is a much better one than that of the Corn Bunting, and is occasionally even a little varied.

Just below, on an alder branch or withy-sapling, sits a fine cock Reed Bunting, whose jet-black head and white neck make him a conspicuous object in spite of the sparrow-like brown of his back and wings. Except in plumage, he is exactly like his relations. He will sit there, as long as you like to stay, and shuffling his feathers, give out his odd tentative and half-hearted song. Like the others he builds on or close to the ground, in this case but a few yards from the rails, and his wife, like theirs, lays eggs streaked and lined in that curious way that is peculiar to Buntings alone. I have not had personal experience of our rarer Buntings, the Ortolan, the Snow Bunting, or even the Cirl Bunting, as living birds; but all the members of this curious race seem to have the characteristics mentioned above in a greater or less degree, and also a certain hard knob in the upper mandible of the bill, which is said to be used as a grindstone for the grain and seeds which are the food of them all in the adult state.

Keeping yet awhile to the railway, let us notice that even the station itself meets with some patronage from the birds. In the stacks of coal which are built up close to the siding, the Pied Wagtails occasionally make their nests, fitting them into some hospitable hole or crevice. These, like all other nests found in or about the station, are carefully protected by the employees of the company. In a deep hole in the masonry of the bridge which crosses the line a few yards below the station, a pair of Great Titmice built their nest two years ago, and successfully brought up their young, regardless of the puffing and rattling of the trains, for the hole was in the *inside*, of the bridge, and only some six feet from the rails of the down line. A little coppice, remnant of a larger wood cut down to make room for the railway, still harbours immense numbers of birds; here for example I always hear the ringing note of the Lesser Whitethroat; and here, until a few years ago, a Nightingale rejoiced in the density of the overgrown underwood.

A Ring-ousel, the only specimen, alive or dead, which I have seen or heard of in these parts, was found dead here one morning some years ago, having come into collision with the telegraph wires in the course of its nocturnal migration.

It was preserved and stuffed by the station-master, who showed it to me as a *piebald Blackbird*.

A little further down the line is another bridge, in which a Blue-tit found a hole for its nest last year; this also was in the inside of the bridge, and close to the up-line. This bridge is a good place from which to watch the Tree-pipit, and listen to its charming song. All down the line, wherever it passes a wood or a succession of tall elms and ashes, these little greyish-brown birds build their nest on or close to the grassy banks, and take their station on the trees or the telegraph wires to watch, to sing, and to enjoy themselves. A favourite plan of theirs is to utter their bright canary-like song from the very top twig of an elm, then to rise in the air, higher and higher, keeping up their energies by a quick succession of sweet shrill notes, till they begin to descend in a beautiful curve, the legs hanging down, the tail expanded and inclined upwards, and the notes getting quicker and quicker as they near the telegraph-wires or the next tree-top. When they reach the perching-place, it ceases altogether. So far as I have noticed, the one part of the song is given when the bird is on the tree, the other when it is on the wing. The perching-song, if I may call it so, is possessed by no other kind of Pipit; but the notes uttered on the wing are much the same with all the species. The young student of birds may do well to concentrate his attention for awhile on the Pipits, and on their near relations, the Larks, and the Wagtails. These three seemed to form a clearly-defined group; and though in the latest scientific classification the Larks have been removed to some distance from the other two, it must be borne in mind that this is in consequence only of a single though remarkable point of difference. Apart from definite structural characters, a very little observation will show that their habits are in most respects alike. They all place their nests on the ground; and they all walk, instead of hopping; the Larks and the Pipits sing in the air, while the Pipits and the Wagtails move their tails up and down in a peculiar manner. All are earth-loving birds, except the Tree-pipit and the Woodlark.

We may now leave the railway, and enter the woodland. Most of the birds that dwell here have been already mentioned; and I shall only mention in passing the Jays, the Magpies, and the Crows, those mischievous and predatory birds, which probably do more harm to the game in a single week of April or May, than the beautiful mice-eating Kestrel does during the whole year. They all rob the nests of the pheasants and partridges, both of eggs and young; and when I saw one day in the wood the bodies of some twenty robbers hung up on a branch, all belonging to these three species, I could not but feel that justice had been done, for it is not only game birds who are their victims. A large increase of these three species would probably have a serious result on the smaller winged population of a wood.

Among the more interesting inhabitants of the wood, there are two species which have not as yet been spoken of in these chapters – the Grasshopper Warbler and the Nightingale. The former has no right to be called a *warbler*, except in so far as it belongs to one of these three families in which all our British 'warblers' are now included. It has no song, properly so called; but no one who has the luck to watch it alive, even without a detailed examination of its structure, will doubt its true relationship to the Sedge-warbler and the Reed-warbler. It is not a water-haunting bird, but still rather recalls the ways of its relations, by choosing deep ditches thickly grown with grass and reeds, and sheltered by bramble-bushes; it seems to need something to climb up and down, and to creep about in; like the sedge-birds, it seldom flies any distance, and one is tempted to fancy that all these species would gradually lose the use of their wings as genuine organs of flight, if it were not for the yearly necessities of migration.

I once had a remarkable opportunity of watching this very curious bird. It was about the beginning of May, before the leaves had fully come out; a time which is very far the best in the year for observing the smaller and shyer birds. Intent on pairing or nest-building, they have little fear, if you keep quiet, and you can follow their movements with a glass without danger of losing sight of them in the foliage. I was returning from a delicious morning ramble through Bruern wood, and was just rounding the last corner of it, where a small plantation of baby saplings was just beginning to put on leaf, when my ear caught the unmistakable 'reel' of this bird. Some other birds of the warbler kind, Wren, Robin, Sedgebird, can produce a noise like the winding-up of a watch, but none of these winds it up with such rapidity, or keep it going so long as the Grasshopper Warbler, nor does any cricket or grasshopper perform the feat in exactly the same way. Our bird's noise – we cannot call it a voice – is like that of a very well-oiled fisherman's reel, made to run at a very rapid rate, and its local name of the 'reel-bird' is a perfectly just and good one.

I was on the outside of a little hedge, and the noise proceeded from the saplings on its further side. In order to see the bird I must get over the hedge, which could not be done without a scrunching and crackling of branches sufficient to frighten away a much less wary bird than this. There seemed, however, to be no other chance of getting a sight of the bird, so through the hedge I went; and tumbled down on the other side with such a disturbance of the branches that I gave up all hope of attaining my object. Great was my astonishment when I saw only a few yards from me a little olive-brown bird creeping through the saplings, which I knew at once to be the Grasshopper Warbler. I then took up a fixed position, the little bird after a minute or two proceeded to do the same, and for some time I watched it with my glass, as it sat on a twig and continued to utter its reel. It was only about ten paces from me, and the field-glass which I carried placed it before me as completely as if it had been in my hands. What struck me most about it was its long supple olive-green neck, which was thrust out and again contracted as the reel was being produced; this being possibly, as I fancy, the cause of the strange ventrilo-quistic power which the bird seems to possess; for even while I watched it, as the neck was turned from side to side, the noise seemed to be projected first in one direction and then in another. The reel was uttered at intervals, and as a general rule did not continue for more than a quarter of a minute, but one spell of it lasted for forty seconds by my watch.

Our interview was not to last very long. It unluckily happened that my little terrier, who accompanies me in all my walks, and is trained to come to heel when anything special is to be observed, had been out of sight when I broke the hedge; and now he must needs come poking and snuffing through the saplings just as if a Grasshopper Warbler were as fair game as a mole or a water rat. Nevertheless, so astonishing was the boldness of this bird that he allowed the dog to hunt about for some time around him without being in the least disconcerted. When at last he made off he retreated in excellent order, merely half flying, half-creeping with his fan-like tail distended, until he disappeared in the thick underwood. I would have taken the dog under my arm and tried for another interview, which no doubt he would have given me, if I had not been obliged to depart in order to catch a train to Oxford. This bird was undoubtedly a male who was awaiting the arrival of the females; just at this time they not only betray themselves more easily by the loudness of their reel, but also are well known to be less shy of showing themselves than at any other period of their stay with us. This is the case with most of our summer migrants. Only a few minutes before I found this bird, I had been watching a newly-arrived cock Nightingale, who had not yet found his mate, and was content to sing to me from the still leafless bough of an oak tree, without any of the shyness he would have shown two or three weeks later.

We have every spring a few pairs of Nightingales in our woods. Except when a wood has been cleared of its undergrowth, they may always be found in the same places, and if the accustomed pair is missing in one it is almost sure to be found in another. The edge of a wood is the favourite place, because the bird constantly seeks its food in the open; also perhaps because the best places for the nest are often in the depth of an overgrown hedge, where the cover is thicker than inside a wood. Sitting on the sunny side of such a wood,

I have often had ample opportunity of hearing and watching a pair: for though always somewhat shy, they are not frightened at a motionless figure, and will generally show themselves if you wait for them, on some prominent bough or bit of railing, or as they descend on the meadow in quest of food.

I am always surprised that writers on birds have so little to say of the beauty of the Nightingale's form and colouring. It is of the ideal size for a bird, neither too small to be noticed readily, nor so large as the somewhat awkwardly built Blackbird or Starling. All its parts are in exquisite proportion; its length of leg gives it a peculiarly sprightly mien, and tail and neck are formed to a perfect balance. Its plumage, as seen, not in an ornithologist's cabinet, but in the living and moving bird a little distance from you, is of three hues, all sober, but all possessing that reality of colour which is so satisfying to the eye on a sunny day. The uniform brown of the head, the wings, and the upper part of the back, is much like the brown of the Robin, a bird which in some other respects strangely resembles the Nightingale; but either it is a little brighter, or the larger surface gives it a richer tone. In both birds the brown is set off against a beautiful red; but this in the Nightingale is only distinct when it flies or jerks the tail, the upper feathers of which, as well as the longer quills, and especially the innermost ones, are of that deep but bright russet that one associates with an autumn morning. And throat and breast are white; not pure white, but of the gentle tone of a cloud where the grey begins to meet the sunshine.

In habit the Nightingale is peculiarly alert and quick, not restless in a petty way, like the fidgety Titmice or the lesser warblers, but putting a certain seriousness and intensity into all it does. Its activity is neither grotesque nor playful, but seems to arise from a kind of nervous zeal, which is also characteristic of its song. If it perches for an instant on the gorse-bush beneath the hedgerow which borders the wood, it jerks its tail up, expands its wings, and is off in another moment. If it alights on the ground, it rears up head and neck like a thrush, hops a few paces, listens, darts upon some morsel of food, and does not dally with it. As it sings, its whole body vibrates, and the soft neck feathers ripple to the quivering of the throat.

I need not attempt to describe that wonderful song, if song it is, and not rather an impassioned recitative. The poets are often sadly to seek about it; Wordsworth at least seems to have caught its spirit:

> 'O Nightingale, thou surely art
> A creature of a fiery heart.'

And Wordsworth, as he tells us in the next stanza, found the cooing of the stock-dove more agreeable to his pensive mind. I never yet heard a Nightingale singing dolefully, as the poets will have it sing; its varied phrases are all given out *con brio*, and even that marvellous *crescendo* on a single note, which no other bird attempts, conveys to the mind of the listener the fiery intensity of the high-strung singer. It is a pity to compare the songs of birds; our best singers, Thrush, Blackbird, Blackcap, Robin and Garden-Warbler, all have a vocal beauty of their own; but it may safely be said that none approaches the Nightingale in fire and fervour of song, or in the combination of extraordinary power with variety of phrase. He seems to do what he pleases with his voice, yet never to play with it; so earnest is he in every utterance – and these come at intervals, sometimes even a long silence making the performance still more mysterious – that if I were asked how to distinguish his song from the rest, I should be inclined to tell my questioner to wait by a wood side till he is fairly startled by a bird that puts his whole ardent soul into his song.

The Nightingale's voice is heard no more after mid-June; and from this time onwards the woods begin to grow silent, especially after early morning. For a while the Blackcap breaks the stillness, and his soft sweet warble is in perfect keeping with the quiet solitude. But as the heat increases, the birds begin to feel, as man does, that the shade of a thick wood is more oppressive than the bright sunshine of the meadows; and on a hot afternoon in July you may walk through the woodland and hardly catch a single note.

But on the outskirts of a wood, or in a grassy 'ride', you may meet with life again. The Tit-mice will come crooning around you, appearing suddenly, and vanishing you hardly know how or whither; Woodpigeons will dash out of the trees with that curious impetuosity of theirs, as if they were suddenly sent for on most pressing business. A Robin will perch on a branch hard by, and startle you with that pathetic soliloquy which calls up instantly to your memory the damp mist and decaying leaves of last November. The Green Woodpecker may be there, laughing at you from an elm, or possibly (as I have sometimes seen him), feeding on the ground, and looking like a gorgeous bird of the tropics.

Other birds of the Woodpecker kind are not common in our woods. The Greater Spotted Woodpecker has only once fairly shown himself to me; the Lesser Spotted Woodpecker, which I have heard country folk call the *French Heckle*, seldom catches the eye, though to judge by the number of stuffed specimens which adorn the parlours of inns and farm-houses, it can by no means be very rare.

There is yet one bird of our woods – or rather of one wood, thickly planted with oaks – of which I have as yet said nothing. I had long suspected his presence in that wood, but my search for him was always in vain. One day in May, 1888, I luckily turned down a little by-path which led me through a forest of young ashes, and brought me out into a wide clearing carpeted with blue-bells and overshadowed by tall oaks. Here I heard a sibilant noise, which in the distance I had taken for the Grasshopper Warbler; though I had had doubts of it, as it was not prolonged for more than two or three seconds. Now also I heard from the thick wood beyond the clearing, a series of plaintive notes, something like those of the Tree Pipit and this stopped me again as I was turning away. I listened, and heard these notes repeated several times, feeling more and more certain each time that I had heard them before in this very wood, and suspected them to be the call-notes of the Wood-warbler, a bird with which strangely enough, I had never had any personal acquaintance.

The sibilant noise was all this time going on close at hand. The wood was comparatively silent owing to the east wind, and I could concentrate my attention on these new voices without distraction. I noticed that the sibilation was preceded by three or four slightly longer and more distinct notes and as this answered to my book-knowledge of the Wood-warbler, I became more and more anxious to see the bird. But he would not let me see him. And then came the puzzling plaintive notes again, as different as possible from the sibilant ones, and it became absolutely necessary to discover whether they were uttered by the same creature.

At last I thought I had made sure of the bird in one particular little thicket not more than ten or twelve yards from me, and crept on as softly as possible out of the clearing into the underwood. Of course the dead twigs crackled under my feet and the branches had to be put forcibly aside, and the voice retreated as I neared it; but pushing on a little further into a small open space, I stopped once more, and then firmly resolved not to move again.

I had a long time to wait. Sometimes the plaintive voice, but oftener the sibilant notes, would be uttered quite close to me, and the singer would stay for some time in the same bush, hidden from my sight but near at hand. And at last, I caught sight of a momentary motion in the leaves not ten yards away from me. A minute later I saw the bird, and knew at once that I had the Wood-warbler before me. There was nothing now to do but to stand motionless and see more of it.

By degrees it seemed to grow used to my presence, and showed itself to me without any sign of alarm. What can be more delightful than to watch in perfect solitude and security the bird you have been looking for so long? There was the yellow throat, the delicate white breast, the characteristic streak over the eye – all plainly visible as he sat facing me; and when he kindly turned his tail to me and preened his feathers, I could see the greenish-brown back, and note the unusual length of wing. Several times, when close to me, he gave utterance to that curious 'shivering' sibilation (to use Gilbert White's apt word), his bill opening wide to give the last shake, his head lifted upwards, the long wings quivering slightly, and the whole body vibrating under the effort. One thing more was needed – a visible proof that the long-drawn plaintive notes were his notes too, and this I had the pleasure of securing by a little more patience. But when my little warbler uttered these notes, his bill was not opened wide, nor did his frame vibrate with any apparent effort; they seemed rather an inward soliloquy or a secret signal (as indeed they were), and always ended up with a short note and a sudden closing of the bill, as if to say, 'All's right, that's well over.'

Then behind me I heard the undoubted double call-note of a warbler, which probably I myself caused the little bird's wife to utter, trespassing as I surely was in the neighbourhood of the nest. It did just cross my mind that I ought to search for that nest, but I gave up the idea almost at once, and bade adieu in peace to my new friends. They had shown themselves to me without fear, and they should have no reason to dislike me.

Beyond the woods where these birds live, we come out on scrubby fields, often full of thistles, and spotted with furze bushes. These fields are the special favourites of the Linnets and Goldfinches; the Linnets are in great abundance, the latter, since the Wild Birds' Act came into operation, by no means uncommon in autumn.

We cannot but pause again and again as we make our way through the gorse and brushwood, for the little Linnet in his full summer dress is hardly less beautiful than the Goldfinch, and all his ways and actions are no less cheering and attractive. The male birds differ much, perhaps according to age, in brilliancy of plumage; but a fine cock Linnet in full dress of crimson breast and crown, white wing-bars and tail-feathers, and chestnut back, is to my thinking as splendid a little bird as these islands can show. I can never forget the astonishment of a companion who hardly knew the bird, when I pointed him out a Linnet in this splendid costume one July day on a Radnorshire hill.

The ground now rises towards the hills which form the limit of our western horizon. On these hills may now and then be seen a few birds which we seldom meet with in the lower grounds, such as the Stonechat, the Brambling, the Wheatear; but as the hills are for the most part cultivated, and abound in woods and brooks, the difference between the bird life of the uplands and the lowlands is not remarkable at any time of the year.

It may be worth while, however, to note down in outline the chief movements of the birds in our district in the course of a single year. In January, which is usually the coldest month in the year, the greater number of our birds are collected in flocks in the open country, the villages only retaining the ordinary Blackbirds, Thrushes, Robins, etc. The winter migrants are in great numbers in the fields, but they and almost all other birds will come into villages and even into towns in very severe weather. In February, villages, orchards, and gardens are beginning to receive more of the bird population, while the great flocks are beginning to break up under the influence of the approach of spring. In March the same process goes on more rapidly; the fields are becoming deserted and the gardens fuller. But meanwhile hedges, woods, thickets and streams are filling with a population from beyond the seas, some part of which penetrates even into the gardens, sharing the fruit trees with the residents, or modestly building their nests on the ground. As a rule, though one of a very general kind, it may be laid down that our resident birds prefer the neighbourhood of mankind for nesting purposes, while the summer migrants build chiefly in the thickets and hedges of the open country; so that just at the time when Chaffinches, Greenfinches, Goldfinches, and a host of other birds are leaving the open country for the precincts of the village, their places are being taken by the new arrivals of the spring. Or if this rule be too imperfect to be worth calling a rule at all (for all the Swallow kind but one British species build in human habitations), it is at least true that if a garden offers ample security for nesting, the proportion of residents to migrants taking advantage of it will be much greater than in a wood or on a heath.

Just as the population of the open country begins to decrease in numbers in early spring, so it increases rapidly in the first weeks of summer. The young broods that have spent their infancy in or near the village now seek more extended space and richer supplies of food, and when the hay is cut, they may be found swarming in all adjacent hedges and on

Poking and snuffing through the saplings

the prostrate swathes, while the gardens are comparatively empty. But before July is over an attentive watcher will find that his garden is visited by birds which were not born and bred there; while the residents are away in the fields, the migrants begin to be attracted to the gardens by the ripening fruits of all kinds. Whitethroats, Willow-warblers, Chiff-chaffs, haunt the kitchen garden for a while, then leave it on their departure for the coast and their journey southwards. After this last little migration, the villages and gardens remain almost deserted except by the Blackbirds and Thrushes, the Robins and the Wrens, until the winter drives the wilder birds to seek the neighbourhood of man once more. Even then, unless the garden be well timbered, they will be limited to a very few species, except in the hardest weather; and it is remarkable how little variety will be found among our winter pensioners – those recipients of out-door relief, who spoil their digestions by becoming greedy over a food which is not natural to them.

This rough attempt to sketch the local migrations of birds must be understood as applying to my own village only, and to gardens which are not surrounded with extensive parks.

Summer Studies of Birds and Books

Summer Studies, *a compilation of lectures, papers and pamphlets written between 1886 and 1894, and supplemented by additional material, was published by Macmillans in 1895.*

As well as the chosen extracts that follow, Fowler included chapters on ornithology in the Alps, bird song, the birds of Aristotle, Gilbert White and his studies of the marsh warbler in Oxfordshire and in Switzerland, which appear in modified form under the heading Kingham Old and New *later in this volume. There is also an engaging memoir on Fowler's wire-haired fox terrier, Billy.*

Unlike A Year with the Birds, Summer Studies *is a book for leisurely reading, to be savoured at a steady pace, allowing time for reflection – a book to dip into after a day in the field.*

Maturity, wisdom, mastery of style – all these ingredients can be found in plenteous measure in Summer Studies.

Getting Ready
A March Day's Diary –
17th March, 1890

The labourers are setting fire to the heaps of weeds

Life in a town is on the whole comfortable, convenient, and warm; but how difficult it is there to get a sight of anything but your street, and a section of a cloudy heaven above it! You must be content to see your sunset caught by a church-steeple; you search in vain for a cross street at the end of which the full blaze in the west can be enjoyed. You would hardly know, but for the weathercock, what wind is blowing, unless, indeed, it be a grim north-easter; for the breeze that blows steadily in the country loses its way at the street corner, and comes twisting round in most uncertain trepidation, trying to get quickly out of this unwholesome labyrinth without regard to its proper direction. And you are quite in the dark as to what that wind is doing in the open country. Our street may be sloppy with a plaster of half-melted snow, while a mile out of the town all is fast bound in frost; and a man may con his books or his accounts unconscious of disturbance, while a full gale is roaring on the distant hill-top.

To get out of a town usually needs something of a struggle, but the struggle does not last long. When the noisy chaos of the station has been left behind, we glide out into the fields with just that sensation of calm that I imagine a duck must feel when it slides softly into the water after a period of waddling and quacking. We can sit back and survey such part of the sky as the window of a railway carriage reveals to us; and almost at once we begin to divine that Nature is getting ready. For here and there, though it is but the middle of March, dark drifting curtains of filmy cloud are driven slantingly along the horizon by a wind from the south; and these are nothing less than the forerunners of April showers. The grass of the meadows is getting green, and the plough-lands are red or ochreous beyond their wont; and as we pass a certain familiar cutting I feel sure that the sweet violets are coming into bloom in the short turf above it.

And when the half-hour of travel is over and we mount to the railway bridge and let our eyes wander in unobstructed freedom round the whole countryside, all these impressions are in an instant verified; Nature is really getting ready for summer, and all things animate and inanimate are at work for her.

A few weeks – nay, a few days ago, as I walked up this same road, everything was still; hardly a human being was to be seen, and the country wore that dull and unvaried look that sunless days in winter always give it. Now there is life and stir all round us. At the inn by the station there is a sale of cattle, and the road is beset with bullocks and pigs, all afflicted with that perverseness which these occasions bring out in them so strikingly, to the detriment of the moral characters of their drivers. From the other side of the hedge comes a subdued chorus of bleating, and now I see that three adventurous lambs, who have passed the age of infancy, have forced their way through a gap, and are trying to see something of the world in a busy high road. No shepherd is near, and I take on myself – and a first delicious taste it is of country life – to drive these children back into their nursery, and to fence up the gap with a stray stick or two out of the hedge. Then, as the road turns sharp and brings me face to face with the village at a half-mile's distance I see black objects crossing the sky in every direction, but moving always either to or from the elms and sycamores that cluster round the church tower. As the leafless trees stand out against the light, every nest is revealed; and I see at once that the same change is going on which we have noticed of late years, that the Rooks are gradually leaving the once favourite elm, and that the competition for the favourite sycamore must be a very trying one this year. The tree is not a big one, but there are a score of nests in its highest branches. It is a middle-aged tree, robust and compact, while the elm, as the Rooks no doubt can guess by its increased swaying in a high wind, is verging towards the evening of its stately, unvexed existence.

A little further up the road, on a warm bank facing the west, I see here and there the golden star of a celandine peeping rather shyly through the grass. Our country is high and rather bleak, and I have known some part of even April pass without a single celandine meeting my eye. When that does happen, I know that the keynote of spring is struck. I must go some way to find primroses or violets, and so it is that I look out for the celandine with far greater interest than for these. It is like the Chiff-chaff among birds; neither is very fashionable, but each is very convincing.

Here are the village allotments, in two valuable fields of a dozen acres in all. Great is the change since I was last here. Then they were a sodden and untidy prairie of old cabbage-stalks, occasionally varied by the ruins of a scarecrow – some old hat or bonnet perched on the top of a pole, sloping westwards to show the prevalence of east winds of late, or a string bedizened with fragments of colourless cloth and ribbon stretched between two crazy sticks. Now these allotments are full of living creatures, all getting something ready. The human beings – women, many of them – have already cleared away most of the cabbage stalks; and now in the sunlight the stretches of freshly-dug earth gleam rich and brown, nay, almost red, where the digging is only just finished. This same earth was in the dead of this damp winter a sodden sticky black crust, beaten hard with rain, and greasy with decaying vegetation; now it is changed and fresh in colour, smell, and touch.

Here too the Rooks are very busy – so intent upon their work of clearing off grubs and worms from the newly-turned soil that they fear neither human beings, with whom at this time of year they seem to feel a fellowship of labour, nor the obsolete scarecrows which they have long treated with contempt. And over the allotments, at a well-maintained height of seventy or eighty feet, the traffic of these black labourers is continuous and worth watching. From their trees they must pass over the allotments, and then over a little valley and stream, to reach a vast extent of ploughland, which in two or three weeks they will be clearing of grubs for their young. At present many are still at work on the nests, and from meadow and ploughland alike they come home slowly, bearing burdens of all kinds, deposit them in the nests, and after a bit of wholesome quarrelling are off again at a far quicker speed. On a rainy day I have timed them each way, and found the return journey always much the slower of the two; and well it may be, if they will persist in carrying articles three feet long, like yonder bird, whose effects to convey himself and a long curved stick through a high wind result in a series of tacks and tumbles ludicrous to behold. Why did he seize it at one end, instead of in the middle?

Let us stroll round the further fields before the sun leaves us; it is quieter there, and we shall hear what birds are singing. The first song we hear is a Chaffinch's, and it is a song about which I have something to say. This bird has indeed for some time been getting its song ready, and now, in all the splendour of spring plumage, is singing it without a mistake all round us; but do not suppose that it has been able to achieve this without hard practice. I have never seen the process described, and even of bird-lovers but few, I fancy, notice it; so it may not be amiss to put it down here. It is usually in the first week of February that I catch the first feeble effort on some sunny morning in the Broad Walk at Oxford; but if the weather is fine I listen even earlier, and this year I heard the welcome sound on 31st January in the same place.

Very fragmentary indeed is it when I first hear it at Oxford. Let me explain it by a comparison which may be startling, but is none the less useful. Some of my younger friends who have learnt a song or two from me know the Chaffinch as 'the bowling bird', because the only strain it can sing resembles the normal action of a bowler at cricket. Two slowish steps, three or four quicker ones, and a delivery made with some effort, describe fairly the bowler's action; two slowish notes, three or four quicker ones, and a jerk or twist of the voice – a quick rise and a fall – also make up the full and normal song of the bird. Now, when the practice is beginning, it is just as if an old bowler who had been laid low, let us say by influenza this sickly season, were to find himself incapable of getting much beyond his first two steps. When he gets into the quicker ones he comes to grief from weakness, and the ball drops from his hand. So with the bird; it is really more from the tone that I divine he is at work, than any recognition of the old familiar strain. But when I have once made sure, I listen and hear him struggling to get on a bit, rushing valiantly at his quick notes perhaps, and only stopping short at the final jerk. If the next morning be fine, I shall no doubt hear even this last crowning glory of his song feebly hinted at; and then, having got so far, an ardent and assiduous bird, who wishes to be beforehand in his courting will sit on the same branch for an hour together and 'bowl' away in the wildest fashion, wide of the net at each delivery, frequently collapsing entirely in the middle of his action, but ever returning to the charge, determined to hit the wicket before he leaves his perch. I have often been the only audience while this has been going on, and once I remember laughing out loud at the absurdity of the performance. To any one who knows well the full and perfect song, there is nothing more comical in nature; yet the bird is very much in earnest, for much of the coming season's happiness may depend on the results of this persistent practice.

Why the Chaffinch should stand almost alone among birds in the trouble he has with his song, is more than I can explain; I know at present but one other whose song is not almost perfect from the first day of singing. If I am to make a guess, it would be that this bird's song is curiously stereotyped to a particular form, which needs an effort each time it is gone through, and that to get it perfect a fair amount of warmth and bodily vigour is necessary; while others, whose musical range is more elastic, can accommodate their voices to their bodily condition without producing ludicrous results. And I may call the Yellow-hammer as a witness to my theory; for he, whose song is also stereotyped in one mould – that which is familiar to us all as 'a little bit of bread and no cheese' – will rarely bring out his 'cheese' in his first spring effort, and is at all times liable to drop it, if he be in a lazy or melancholy mood.

Other birds are singing – Thrushes, Robins, Dunnocks, Wrens, Greenfinches; whose voices already perfect in execution, need no comment. Let us notice what else is getting ready, in these fields that slope down to the brook. The Starlings seem to be in a state of transition, as becomes them about the equinox; of course they have been getting ready for weeks, but some at least of them stick to their habits of the winter, for there are flights of them hurrying westward to their roosting-place beyond the hills, where the sun will soon be setting. Birds that can still do this have hardly yet begun to nest.

It is really in the grass and the ploughland that I see most change since my last visit. This meadow slopes before me to the west, and the sun, now close on the hill-top, fills all the grass with light, making the old brown tufts stand out distinctly amid the fresh growth of today. Those old tufts remind me of snow, and of Keat's hare that 'limped trembling through the frozen grass'; these warm, green patches, of the boundless growth of buttercups that is to come, of exhausted cows on a hot June day, of all that wealth of summer rain that no farmer seems to be able to foretell and anticipate. Thought might wander on at will, but my eye catches a new token of business (in the real sense of that sorrily-handled word) in the abundant mole-heaps that crowd the slope a little farther on.

These indefatigable little animals have been at work since January, when their favourite hunting-grounds suddenly showed an eruption of little brown hillocks; every morning shows a fresh eruption. In spite of the worst deluges we ever suffer there, the moles are on the spot again as soon as ever the water has cleared away. I have often wandered up and down the valleys, noticing the lie and order of the mole-heaps in the meadows; and find that these wary creatures do not often trust themselves out of reach of all means of retreat to higher ground. They live for the most part in those pleasant gently-sloping fields that lie just above the flat alluvial meadows; and here or in the adjoining hedgerows you find their winter homes – huge mounds with a convenient series of passages, and with a warm nest of cut grass in a large chamber deep down in the centre. Hence they issue forth on hunting expeditions after worms in the water-meadows; for worms and water are their two chief wants. Once or twice I have found their fortresses in what at first looked a perilous spot, in the flat ground close to a stream; but never in any place constantly liable to flood. And here, where we stand now, looking down on the little green valley with its brook, I can clearly distinguish the parts where the water is apt to lie for a day or two in wet weather, by the entire absence of mole-heaps.

And now the sun is behind the hill, and we will turn

homewards by the path that skirts this ploughed field, whose freshly-harrowed surface shows red lights and shadows in the sunset, reminding me of the coat of a little red Devonshire cow. The deeps and hollows in that almost furry coat have a way of treating the sunshine which was a constant pleasure to me when staying at an Exmoor farmhouse; and here is the same rough broken surface, changed from brown to various reds by the sunset behind me. Still more magical is the work of the sunset on the blue smoke that is now rising in every direction from the allotments, when the labourers are setting fire to the heaps of weeds they have been collecting. It drifts away with the evening breeze, and spreads over the whole land; and then, as the sun sets, a wonderful transformation scene takes place. All outlines lose their clearness; all strong colours become subdued; all objects are seen through a soft veil of pale violet, which clothes the whole countryside in such a tissue of quiet russets and lilacs as I will not attempt to describe. It is this weed-burning which makes the dullest open country so beautiful in sunny evenings of March and September, and always forbids me to shut up my windows until the light has almost vanished, and I can see nothing but a flame breaking out here and there from a heap whose moisture has at last been exhausted in smoke.

18th March – Another beautiful and sunny morning, though the wind is veering round to the east. A stroll through the fields brings me to a hedge which has lately been lopped; the superfluous branches are lying on the grass in bundles. It is one of our warmest spots, and I am always on the look-out for birds there. I have just been watching those birds of winter, the fieldfares, gathered in numbers on some trees, and chattering excitedly as if they were about to leave us. Suddenly a little brown thing flits out of one of the bundles of branches, hovers a minute in the air, and returns to shelter. There is not a bird among all our winter residents that would flit into the air like that, nor one that would creep among the twigs exactly as he is creeping now. Out he comes again, plays in the air for a second, and alights on another bundle a few yards further on. I have no longer any doubt, but my glass makes assurance doubly sure; it is the Chiff-chaff, the first of our summer birds, the first traveller to reach us from Africa and the warm south. He seems to have divined that we have been early in getting ready for him, and has accepted our invitation at an earlier date than I ever remember in these uplands. He has probably come up the valley, following the windings of the stream, where he can always find both insects and shelter. At this point he has left it, and is making his way up the hedges till he arrives at his last year's home, where he can await the later arrival of a bride; soon his merry double note will be heard from elm or wood-side, announcing that all is ready for her.

The superfluous branches lying on the grass in bundles

Among the Birds in Wales

There is a valley stretching far away into the wildest moorland

In the flat meadows of the midlands, with their deep alluvial soil, there is a certain lush richness of vegetation in June which makes the air heavy and languid. Unless the weather chances to be unusually dry and bright, you cannot push through even a few yards of that dense herbage without feeling the moisture that lurks in the depths of it; the same moisture that becomes visible, when the sun goes down, in a white film of vapour which rises ghost-like in the dusk, and covers the meadows like a sheet, ending exactly where the hedge divides the upward-sloping pasture-field from the growing hay of the flat ground.

It is at this time, before the hay is cut and the damp of the grass-roots is exposed and dried, at the very time when the flowers are most brilliant, and the gently-flowing water of our streams lingers lazily about the yellow flags and blue geraniums that fringe the banks – it is in the very height of the glory of midland verdure that I always feel a strong desire after light air and short grass. To mount to some height overlooking the plain, where in an old quarry the rock has been overgrown with thyme, or where on the broad strips of grass that border the road some remnants are still left of the old flora of the downland, is to me at this time always a delight and a relief. Should there chance to be a corner where a few tufts of heather still linger among the furze-bushes, and where perhaps a little copse of pines varies the almost wearisome landscape of hedgerow elms and growing crops, then it is pleasant to lie for a while and listen to the Linnets or watch the handsome Stonechat, picturing to oneself the time when half England was like this little nook, and when no one delighted in his wealth of wilderness as I do in this scanty remnant.

But for those who can get a holiday in June it is possible to go farther away from heavy air and sleepy days than to the top of the neighbouring hills. In June the Alps are clothed in their wealth of flowers, and every breath of air is laden, not with rich sweet odours, but with dry, invigorating, aromatic deliciousness; and many a time have I made my pilgrimage thither, to find the short grass I long for, still uneaten by the cows, and gay with a thousand blooms. Quite as enjoyable, and less far to seek, is the still shorter grass of the chalk downs of southern England; for there the light air comes from the sea; though not iced, it is fresh with the salt water; and as it breathes through the long bents and gathers the fragrance of the thyme, it dries up every tiny drop of moisture that has not already sunk into the porous soil, and gives you free leave to throw yourself without a thought of consequences on the grass, within an hour or two after a scudding shower has refreshed the thirsty down.

One languid June, when duties came to an end at Oxford,

it so happened that I could not seek the light air and short grass I longed for, either in the Alps or on the downs; and it was only an accident that took me for three or four days to a hospitable house in the Welsh hills, where I found all I needed. It was a district offering little of the 'striking scenery' which attracts the tourist, and he is almost unknown in these parts; there is in fact no accommodation for him. During a six week's stay in the wildest part of these hills some twenty years ago, working hard and trying to beguile unwilling trout, I saw but one pair of tourists. You may walk for miles over high wet moorland and never strike a track; you may very easily lose yourself and follow down some brook which, with a gradual curve, will take you in the opposite direction to the point you wish to make for. And if rain and mist come on, as they did one summer evening years ago, when I was crossing from valley to valley by an ill-defined track, you may find a pocket compass a deliverance from a very comfortless night.

It was nearly twenty years since I had been in these hills, and they, or rather I should say, all the *details* of them, were as good as new to me. I noticed with curiosity how these details gradually came back to me as things known in a previous state of existence, bringing the old associations back with them. Again and again their original writing on my mind had been written over, in other regions and other climates, and yet by some mysterious process it was brought to light, and the palimpsest made intelligible. In ascending one hill through a wood, I could not be sure that I was on the old familiar path till certain mossy rocks, jutting out into the path under the ash-trees, came home to me like old friends – not suddenly, but with a growing consciousness of certainty that became firmer every minute. I sat down a while by those old rocks to let them have their way with me.

In those days I knew nothing of birds; I was far too much engrossed in Aristotle and fishing to find something new to learn, for birds are everywhere; and in this very spot I had a note to make that was of great interest to me. In the Alps I have noticed that the song of the Tree-pipit is heard in all the lower timbered pastures up to the point at which the pines come to an end, and the real alps begin. To that point you must ascend if you would hear the true Alpine Pipit, which there takes the place of the other, singing perhaps a more monotonous song but one quite as blithe and cheering, as it hovers in the air out of sight, then slowly nears you, to drop on to a boulder or a tuft of alpine rhododendron. During my short climb up the Welsh hill-side I had heard the Tree-pipit continually, and when I reached the margin of the wood and came out on those delicious gentler slopes, where only a tree here and there breaks the welcome sky-line, the same bird was still singing vigorously; but as soon as I had left these straggling trees behind me, and was fairly out on the open moorland of sweet short grass and thick dry ling, then I was saluted by the voice, not of the alpine bird, but of our own English Meadow-pipit, which descends in autumn, like its alpine cousin, to lower feeding grounds, and is known in fact to all of us, at all seasons, as the Titlark. The bird soon catches your eye, and hovers near you if you are likely to approach its nest; no mystery attends it, no great mountain walls encompass it, nor does it mount far away in air and 'despise the earth' like the Skylark that was singing there too, away from all human cultivation, a tiny speck against the light driving clouds.

There is a valley in this district, stretching far away into the wildest moorland, of which the alpine character is quite unmistakable. The hills rise steeply from the swiftly-flowing river, and are in many places clothed with dense plantations of pine and larch; above these again you come out on yet steeper slopes of grass and fern, with grey silurian rock jutting out in regular lines, or sometimes forming precipices intersected by damp mossy gullies, difficult indeed to climb, but leading to that invigorating level moorland where the Pipits have their summer home.

The Ring-ousel nests not far off, and we can now and then hear his metallic alarm-note from some stunted bush among the crags. Here too is of course the Wheatear, singing that delicate warble which is so grateful to the ear of the dweller in midland plains; and here too are a few pairs of Redstarts, reminding us of those darker cousins of theirs which welcome us to the highest alpine pastures.

What Englishman would naturally think of our little Redstart as a bird of the mountains? We associate him in Oxfordshire, where he abounds in ever-increasing numbers, with the thick hedgerow, the pollards by the lazy stream, the old wall in the garden, the chequered shade of the orchard. Yet his tastes seem to be almost as cosmopolitan as those of his continental cousin, – modified, I should perhaps add, with some slight tincture of caprice. It is most strange that in the south-east of England he should be comparatively uncommon. Ten days of constant walking in Kent showed me hardly a single pair, and confirmed all that had been told me by residents in that county and Sussex. If we are to try and explain why it should prefer the west to the east, I should be inclined to guess that the waterless downs and heaths do not suit its needs so well as damp river-valleys and moist mountain sides. The Redstart loves the pollard willows that line our midland streams, and all places where good nesting-holes, and abundant insect food, and plentiful water can be found; and no one who is used to see him daily and hourly in such places would expect to find him in equal plenty in a drier climate.

But to return to the Welsh hills. Here in June it is still spring; such hedges as there are here are still white with hawthorn blossom, and the wild roses have hardly begun to bloom. The grass even here in the valley is short enough for me: a short, thick undergrowth of flowers, with enough of taller grasses to suggest that it is meant for hay. But about these fields, and at the junction of two mountain streams, the Sand-martins are busy, reminding me of the richer water-meadows I have left behind me in England. The Sand-martins took me by surprise: in old days I never noticed them, and never learnt to associate them with water that talks as it runs. About Oxford, where they are perhaps in greater numbers than in any other haunt of mine, their conversation is unbroken by the noise of the water; and in the silence of a still summer evening it forces itself on your attention, for there is nothing but your own thoughts to rival it. Here, with the streams and the Sand-martins chatting all around me, there seemed to be much more life and stir than by the silent Thames in the heavy English air. Probably this was the last colony on this side of the mountain range which separated me from the Irish Sea: the last ripple of the wave of Sand-martins which comes surging in April up the larger rivers, breaking into lesser parties, we may suppose, to seek old haunts up the smaller streams, and so touching with one of its last laps this far-away mountain hamlet.

In 1869, when I spent some weeks in one of these valleys, the cry of the Buzzards was the daily accompaniment to our studies of Aristotle and Livy. In 1894, a few miles from the same spot, it was still possible to lie on the crest of a hill and watch two, three, or even four of these noble birds soaring overhead at the same time. Ravens I do not remember in the old days, but of ornithology I then knew nothing. In the spring of the present year they were numerous, and many a sickly lamb on the mountains had his young eyes hacked out by those terrible bills of theirs. While scanning the un-clouded blue for even grander birds than these, I once caught myself saying, as a black speck over the opposite hill began to near us, 'It's only a Raven!' And this in spite of all the farmer's temptations to destroy this cruel enemy of his. The Raven will not easily be extirpated; there are still English counties as well as Welsh ones in which he may be hopefully looked for, and if the passion for private egg-collecting can be only kept within due bounds, there need be no fear that he will disappear from our British list. I have a record, in a diary kept among these hills in 1869, of the appearance of a Kite for two successive days; and since then, though always expected to die out, these comparatively harmless hermits have contrived to maintain themselves here. This year almost in the same spot where I first saw them a quarter of a century ago, I once more watched their magnificent flight with wondering eyes. Few Englishmen have had that experience, and some may care to read the note I made. 'We soon saw a Kite above us, at first quite near; the sun lit up the red colour of his back and tail, and (as he turned) the rusty feathers of his under parts. The wings were narrow, with the primaries standing out distinct from each other like a Crow's; the tail long, the "fork" most distinct – as if a deep segment of a circle had been cut out of it. My companion was just saying that this might be the last survivor of the race, when a second bird appeared rising from the wood to our left, and then soared just over our heads, giving us a splendid view. The two then circled in a slow upward flight: the wings beaten eight to twelve times in succession, with a curving motion of the wing, then a graceful glide round half or more of the circle. At last they became mere specks in the blue, and we could hardly keep them in view even with a strong field-glass.'

These splendid birds were then engaged upon a nest in a place very far indeed from being inaccessible. I need not say that we left that nest wholly undisturbed, and that we bound ourselves to betray the secret of the spot to no one. Yet when next I had news of the district the harpies had descended upon it, though whether they robbed the Kites' nest I know not, but they wrought other havoc. From what I saw two months later I am inclined to hope that the Kites retreated to a position from which even an egg-dealer would have found it hard to dislodge them, and that their life's last breeding season may after all have been a happy one. But let me insist on it once more that, though they may escape the farmer and the sportsman, neither of whom is in those parts wantonly vindictive, they cannot long survive the greed of the trader in eggs; and further that the trader himself can only be suppressed by a rigid self-denying ordinance on the part of the private collector.

But we must leave the rocky summits of the hills, and descend, perhaps through very steep woodland, to the winding valley with its road and river. In some places the hills are clad almost to the very crown with trees; and not only with pine or larch, but here and there with oaks of no great height, with a border of ashes or sycamores on their last gentler mossy slopes by the river. Beneath the trees is no great luxuriance of grass, for the brake-fern here has it all its own way, and covers the whole hill-side, except where an occasional bit of rock juts out, in the shelves and crannies of which a mossy turf is spread. Could any place be a more pleasant and beautiful home for wood-loving birds? I have often noticed that a steep slope, where the trees are not too closely packed for the sun to shine freely in among the shadows, is always a favourite haunt. Was there not, and is there not, the famous Hanger of Selborne made memorable for ever to English bird-lovers? Another such steep wood in the chalk country has been admirably described by the late Mr. Jefferies in the *Gamekeeper at Home*. They are good for bird-observers as well as for birds, for there is no position as happy as one from which you can look *down*, unobserved, through a vista of trees, without wearying the eyes by a long, strained, upward search through tangled foliage. Taking up your position at some point where you can command as many trees as possible, leaving the upper and denser foliage for the most part out of your thoughts, but keeping a keen eye on all barer boughs or leafless twigs – for these are specially affected by some birds, and others too will come to them in the course of their wanderings, – you may sit quietly down and wait, with binocular ready, and ear as keenly observant. In such moments the sharp look-out you have to keep will in no way hinder you from enjoying the beauty of the interlacing oak-branches, or the grey tint which the lichen that everywhere clings to them gives to the whole woodland scene.

The ear will probably be the first watchman to give the signal for a still closer attention. The voices of the ubiquitous Chaffinch and Willow-wren have not been enough to rouse it, for they are at hand everywhere, both in Wales and England. But now I hear the voice of a little bird that is not too common to be invariably attractive and interesting; it is not unlike the winding-up of an old-fashioned watch or a musical box, if you imagine the key turned very slowly at first, then more and more quickly, until the position of the

winder's hand compels him to rest for a moment and begin
the operation afresh. A most curious voice is his, and though
not strictly musical, very far from unpleasing to the ear; the
silvery 'shivering' quality of it which White noticed long ago
has a way of craving your attention, and growing upon you
as it comes nearer and nearer. Patience is necessary if we
would see the bird fairly; and the only way is to sit and wait
till you have caught him, even but for an instant, with your
unassisted eye, and marked the tree in which he is searching
for food. He will not wander far, unless you pursue him; the
nest is in the fern not far away, and the persistence of his note
makes it probable that his wife is still sitting on eggs, and
that the duty of finding food for hungry young has not yet
begun. Watch him till he comes near enough to show you
how all a bird's mind is put into his song; as he utters it his
long, closed wings are slightly opened and shaken, and his
bill opens wider and wider, till the vibrating tongue is clearly
visible as the head is held upwards to sustain the effort.
Every now and then he will communicate with his wife by a
signal she knows well: it is a series of long, pathetic notes,
which can be heard at a long distance, and speak his tender
love and appreciation of her labours. These notes are uttered
– for I have watched the bird at a distance of a few feet – with
the bill almost closed, and with no sign of effort; they are
rather an inward meditation than an outspoken call, in spite
of their resonance.

What you see when the Wood-wren has revealed himself
is nothing but a little brown bird with a whitish-yellow
throat and pure white breast and belly; the books indeed tell
you that there is much yellow about it, but this you would
readily discover only if you had it in your hand and could
turn up the feathers. But if not conspicuous in his colouring,
he is a model of perfect grace in shape and movement; and if
birds are to be studied, as indeed I hope they are, not merely
as empty skins, but as living creatures with minds, hoping
and fearing, rejoicing and sorrowing, here is one that I may
well watch for half an hour, and feel as much indebted to the
sight of his delicate form and harmonious motion as I should

to the contemplation of the gracefullest of Greek vases or the purest melody of Mozart.

There is one other bird which I should wish to notice before I leave these woods, one which does not need to be watched for like the Wood-wren, but obtrudes himself upon your attention by his bright plumage, his comparatively loud note of warning, and his preference for the lower and barer boughs of the trees. It is not often that we of the midlands have the chance of seeing or hearing a Pied Flycatcher. When he does appear, he is only a passing visitor on his way to the hills, and I have never known him stay with us more than one day. Yet it is well to keep a look-out for him in the valleys of the Thames and its affluents during the latter half of April; and his plumage is just then so brilliant that it cannot fail to catch the eye. The white of the breast is so pure that in the sunshine it will be distinctly visible at a great distance, and can be distinguished at once from the greyer tint of the same parts in the commoner species. I have on two or three occasions come upon a pair travelling together in Oxfordshire or rather resting from their travel; they perch on a railing and spend the day in catching flies with such an air of contentment that you are deluded into fancying that they are going to remain your guests; but the next day you will look for them in vain.

It would seem that the flat country is not to the mind of this bird, and he quickly leaves our gardens and orchards to the Spotted Flycatchers who are following him from the Continent, and makes north and west for wooded hills and dales. Perhaps his favourite homes are the central hills of Wales. Even here, however, he is somewhat capricious; for while in Breconshire and Radnorshire he is quite a common bird, I have never once found him in the Glamorganshire hills, which I have known almost all my life. On the Continent I have always seen him in just such places as he loves in Wales, among the larger timber of a Swiss mountain-side, or on the forest slopes of the Taunus range. Just as the trout loves swiftly-running streams, or as the Wood-wren is sure to be heard where the oak is the prevailing tree, so there are certain spots which you instinctively feel that this bird ought to have chosen for his habitation, and if you are in the right district you may fairly lay a wager that he will be found there.

Such a spot, on the edge of the beech forests of Wiesbaden, will always remain in very clear outline in my memory, for it was there I first heard the song of this bird. It is very seldom now that I hear a song that is quite new to me. If it were not that so many of our songsters sing all too short a time, and that when they tune up one by one for the orchestra of the spring season each instrument touches the ear with the fresh delight of recognition, I might feel as much at the end of my tether as the mountaineer who has no more peaks to climb. But this song was not only new, but wonderfully sweet and striking. 'Something like a Redstart's,' say the books, and this is not untrue, so far as it represents the outward form, so to speak, of the song – the quickness or shortness of notes, the rapid variations of pitch. But no one who has once accustomed his ear to the very peculiar *timbre* of the voice of either kind of Redstart will mistake for it the song of the Pied Flycatcher. My notes taken on the spot, and before I had seen any other description of it, recall the song to my memory – the short notes at the beginning, the rather fragmentary and hesitating character of the strain, and the little *coda* or finish, which reminded me of the Chaffinch; but all this will have no meaning to my readers. There is but one way of learning a bird's song, and that is by listening to it in solitude again and again, until you have associated it in your mind with the form and habits and haunts of the singer.

The Pied Flycatcher may, under certain circumstances, be a puzzling bird to the novice. An old male, in full plumage of black and white, is indeed unmistakable; but the female, the young, and (as is now well known) some at least of the birds of a year old, have the back and head of a greyish brown. The pair which I watched at Wiesbaden were very much alike, and as they were flitting about the highest branches of an old gnarled oak, I had some trouble in identifying them even with the field-glass. I knew little of the species then, and the brown in both sexes puzzled me, the song puzzled me, and when the male showed his tail to me delightfully while clinging Swift-like to the mouth of the hole they were choosing for their nesting-place, the white of the two outer tail-feathers puzzled me no less. Worst of all, the brown of the head was distinctly reddish, and it was not for some time that I discovered that this was caused by the sunlight falling on the bird and reflected through the ruddy young oak-leaves that brilliant April morning. Only the *manner* of the birds and the peculiar pose of their heads kept me pretty steadily to the conviction that I had Flycatchers before me.

A few years ago it was hardly known that this beautiful bird is so regular a visitor to many parts of Wales; but recently some attention has been paid to Welsh birds, and good ornithologists are at work there. I should not be surprised, were I to live long enough, to find that some remarkable discoveries had been made among those wilder hills which the tourist has not found out, and where the smaller birds are despised or overlooked by the sportsman. For myself, I confess that when among these hills, the evil propensities of former days are apt to get the better of me, and by a deep, dark pool, well ruffled by the mountain breeze, I almost cease to hear the note of the Wood-wren coming towards me through the lichened oak-boughs, while I extract one little trout after another from the peaty water. I could almost wish that, like these Wood-wrens, the trout had a voice to express his hopes and fears; if that were so, I think my fishing career would once more be a thing of the past. It may be that one reason at least why of all sports fishing is the only one that pleases me is because a fish is a silent animal. You haul him from his element – he complains not but by gesture; you put a speedy end to his existence by a sharp knock – he leaves his life indignant but in silence. There is a certain tarn among these hills where the trout are said, when caught, to give vent to their indignation in inarticulate sounds; but I have never fished in that pool, nor, if I found the story true, would I fish there a second time.

A Chapter on Wagtails

Were I condemned to a desert island, I should wish to have some birds, as well as books

Were I condemned to live on a desert island, I should wish to have some birds, as well as books, for my companions. Among books I should need some few of those that abound in such choice detail as will easily slip off the mind, and as easily be recalled and enjoyed at the next *perusal* – a good old word, by the way, which cannot be applied to the reading of every book. *Boswell, The Vicar, Jane Austen, Elia*, are of this kind; we can *peruse* them, – the page lies open a while for leisurely enjoyment, and is not feverishly turned. I would have birds too that can be perused; not hasty ones that are up and away the moment they catch sight of you, nor huge ones, sailing solemnly over your head and vanishing over the hill while you adjust your glass. I would have little ones that come and go regardless of you, dallying about close at hand, pursuing their avocations while you sit and watch them with the same fresh interest that drew you to them twenty years ago. I would have Warblers, Redstarts, Flycatchers, or better still, the Wagtails.

It is impossible ever to weary of Wagtails. We are never altogether without them, yet whenever they present themselves to us we are constrained to give them our attention. Some birds you can glance at as you walk and talk, but no sooner does a Wagtail alight on the path in front of you than he compels you to pause, and look at him carefully. There are, indeed, scientific reasons why Wagtails should always be noticed; but apart from these there is a never-failing pleasure in contemplating their symmetry of form, their beauty of colouring, their graceful flight, their unobtrusive confidence, and that constant unresting activity of theirs – an activity which some mysterious grace of mental build never suffers to degenerate into fidgetiness.

There are Wagtails in most parts of the world, and from Britain eastwards to Japan they are abundant, puzzling the ornithologist with their endless varieties of plumage, and utterly declining to be neatly and finally classified. The whole group, it is true, is perfectly well defined, if not by structure, at least by outward appearance, habit, and motion; but the species within the group run into each other in a way which seems to be as baffling as it is instructive. No family of birds has more to tell us of the nature and growth of species; but none needs more careful handling, more laborious investigation and travel. Into this labyrinth, however, I am not competent to venture; I may refer once or twice to two species which are, strictly speaking, Continental, but I shall have enough to say, without travelling further, about the three which habitually breed in our island.

These three are – first, the Pied Wagtail, commonly known as the Water Wagtail or Dishwasher, the black and white bird which we all know so well; next, the Yellow Wagtail of the pasture meadows and lazy streams, which comes to us in spring and leaves us in autumn; thirdly, the so-called Grey Wagtail of the mountain brooks and rivers, which can always be distinguished from the others by its very long tail. All these three resemble each other closely in their habits, as well as in their build. They all love the neighbourhood of water; they all have the same peculiar flight – a graceful flight, consisting of successive upward and downward curves, which enables us to detect them even at a long distance. They all have the same quality of voice – a short and shrill musical whistle, which cannot be confused with the note of any other bird, unless it be indeed with that of their nearest relations the Pipits. They all move their tails gently up and down, build their nests on or close to the ground, and lay eggs of which the ground-colour is nearly always a pale, bluish white, spotted more or less with brown or grey. They all walk, or rather run, instead of hopping, their delicate little legs being often in such swift motion as hardly to be seen as they go; and all feed chiefly on insects – largely, I think, on minute beetles – and love our British streams and meadows for the never-failing abundance of food they find there. And I should add that in all our three birds the two outer tail-feathers are white, and become conspicuous the moment their owner flies or moves his tail in the familiar way.

These are the generic peculiarities of the group, and, as far as I know, they are common to all true Wagtails. But our three British species, though they are alike in so many ways, and are without doubt all descended from a single ancestral type, have developed features which mark them off very clearly from each other. The colouring for example, is so distinct in the plumage of the adult male birds in breeding dress, as to be recognised at once even by the inexperienced; and it is interesting to find that they then represent three several types of the world's Wagtails. One is black and white, with a jet-black gorget; one is yellow and olive-brown, with no black at all; and the third, which stands between the two, though I take him last in this chapter, is grey above, bright yellow beneath, and has the same black throat ornament as his Pied cousin. Our British Wagtails, then, are well worth careful study; for, however far an inquirer may travel in quest of Wagtails, he is not likely to find any which do not come near to one of these three types.

Let us begin with the black and white bird; him at least we can hardly fail to find at any time of the year. But where shall we look for him? Not necessarily by the brook-side; but if a farmyard pond is at hand, or a bit of shallow in the stream – a miniature ford, perhaps, with stepping stones – you may do well to give a glance there. In spring or autumn try a field which is being ploughed; the first field the farmer turns is sure to have its Pied Wagtails. If they chance to be on migration they will collect there to enjoy the minute creatures which the plough exposes, and you may see scores and even hundreds of them hard at work together. The chance will be a good one, if it be autumn, for noting the variety of plumage in both old and young, and for making so sure of this bird that you can never mistake him for his whiter cousin of the Continent. In the breeding season a freshly-mown lawn has a great attraction for him; the meadow grass is then either growing to hay or getting so thick and coarse that it is not easy to find the insects in it. I fancy too that all Wagtails like to use their little legs freely, unhampered by thick stalks of crowded herbage; on a lawn they can see insects at a distance, and run with sudden spurts, half flying too sometimes, to seize them. While eating and while running the tail is mostly still; but no sooner is the run over and a fresh morsel pounced on, than it is moved up and down rapidly, showing plainly the two outer white feathers.

But his nest may be some distance away from the lawn he patronises, and we are not likely to find it unless we have ample time to watch. This bird is very apt to choose odd places, and many stories have been told of his caprice in this way. Caprice it may indeed seem to us, but I cannot but think it has an object – to escape the constant persecution of the Cuckoo. It was for this reason, I am sure, that a pair in the garden of a friend of mine built a nest in the far recesses of a greenhouse among the flowerpots. This nest was a singular one, and must have cost the birds infinitely more labour than usual; for as it was not fitted into any hole, or supported by anything but the shelf on which it stood, a strong substructure had to be built first, on which it could securely rest. The mass of dry grass and moss was quite wonderful, and all the more pity that it should have been collected in vain. The pair escaped from one enemy only to fall victims to another. The Cuckoo found them out, but was herself found out by the gardener before she had actually deposited her egg; and all might have gone well if a cat had not strayed that way. That the Cuckoo should have followed the birds into the greenhouse just at the time when all was ripe for its mischief – for there were then four eggs in the nest – seems to me to show that it had been watching this pair of birds for some time; this the Wagtails well knew, and, abandoning perhaps their original intention, chose this unlikely place.

Curious fondness of this bird for railway stations

I think this must also be the explanation of that curious fondness of this bird for railway stations. When I say that almost every country station has its pair, I am not going very much beyond the facts. Here at Kingham it has been so ever since I began to notice birds; the familiar little double note from the station roof is so well known to me that I now barely stop to notice it. At one time they used to build in the crevices of the stacks of coal; this year there was a nest almost under the signal-box, and just beneath the massive wooden posts fixed at the end of a siding to resist the force of shunted trucks. They are conspicuous birds, and the Cuckoo would soon find them out if they gave her a fair chance; but the bustle of men and trains perhaps deters her.

When the nesting time is over, the parents and their young broods, after spending the day on lawn or meadow, will associate in roosting in some convenient cover. But the autumn is the time to look out for their great gatherings. Then they travel in multitudes, hardly observable by day, when they are often on the newly-ploughed fields, but if you should happen to come upon them at nightfall, fairly astonishing you with their numbers. One day in early October, I strolled at sunset down to the meadow of which part is occupied by the osier bed that first attracted the Marsh Warbler; it was fast getting dark, but I at once heard the shrill double notes all round me. All along the stream I put Pied Wagtails up at every step; then turning up to the railway which runs above the field, I saw the telegraph wires covered with them. With the help of the glass I counted forty-five on the wires and another forty on the grass just below them; then I went to the osier-bed and threw a stone into it, which brought out a cloud of wagtails, disturbed from their first sleep.

The next time I was able to pay this wonderful field a visit there was only a pair or two to be seen, and I have no doubt that this great gathering meant migration. We have abundant evidence that the Pied Wagtail passes over to the Continent in great numbers in the autumn, though there are always enough left behind to let us feel that they are still with us. Some years ago an old friend of mine, a master at Westward Ho! College in North Devon, wrote to me just at the end of September describing a strange immigration of Pied Wagtails which had occurred there a day or two before. It was a warm evening, and the windows of the large school building, which fronts the sea, were open, and the lights within were of course visible out at sea. Suddenly the rooms were invaded by a host of Pied Wagtails, which swarmed in, circling round and round the ceiling like bats, and so distracted that they could be caught with butterfly nets. On this same coast of North Devon parties may be seen in the autumn making progress towards the west, to cross the county to the southern coast, where they seem to congregate for further travel.

We can trace this travel, and find that it is now directed towards the *east*. On the coast of Dorset I have seen them gathered in vast numbers in late September; somewhat further eastward they cross the Channel, and some at least then go southward along the French coast, for we catch a glimpse of them again in Portugal. Once arrived on the Continent, they must find themselves comparative strangers: for though they are among their own kin, the White Wagtails, they do not seem to be always received with the hospitality due to near relations. Yet these two species – incomplete they may be as species, yet something more than mere races or varying forms – will sometimes associate, and even mate, together. The White Wagtail, which is a pretty constant visitor to this country in spring, may sometimes find himself (or herself) without a mate, and take up with a Pied Wagtail in default of his own kind. But the endless varieties of Wagtail plumage, in old and young, and male and female, at different times of the year, must be left to those who have time and materials for a close and accurate study.

When the Pied Wagtail was first distinguished by naturalists from its Continental cousins, it received the unfortunate name of Motacilla lugubris, or the Wagtail in mourning, in allusion to its black and white dress. To give such a name to such a bird is to forget that he is something more than an arrangement in feathers; I do not think that a Wagtail could look mournful even under the most painful circumstances. No such misfortune, I am glad to say, has happened to the Yellow Wagtail, the sprightliest, boldest, and perhaps the happiest, of its kind. It has often been called, in Latin as well as English, simply the Yellow Wagtail; but the greater number of authors have given it, in a Latin form the name of the great English naturalist John Ray, and even in common speech we often speak of it as Ray's Wagtail.

A Chapter on Wagtails

It received this honourable name some half a century ago, because it was then first discovered that, like the Pied Wagtail, it is almost peculiar to Britain, and is quite distinct from the common Yellow Wagtail of the Continent. Here is one of those curious involved bird-mysteries which make the science of ornithology more fascinating the more our knowledge of it advances. And, to add to our perplexity, few seem to come to us every year; and just as it is worth while always to look at Pied Wagtails to make sure that they are not White Wagtails, so it is as well to glance at all yellow birds we see, in case we should some day meet with one that has a distinctly bluish head, and a white stripe over the eye instead of a yellow one. A beginner, indeed, may easily confuse the female of the common species for the rarity he is looking out for; and he should never be satisfied until he has watched his bird at a very short distance, and if possible with a good field-glass. Though Oxford is a favourite haunt of Yellow Wagtails, I have in the course of many years detected but two or three of the rarer species.

These most charming birds come to Oxford about the middle of April. They come up the river, and gather in great numbers on that vast meadow above the city known as Port Meadow. Here, on the 26th April, 1887, I saw a more wonderful gathering of Yellow Wagtails than I have ever seen since, or am likely ever to see again. I had been told of some Dunlins on the bank of the Isis, where it bounds this great meadow to the west. As these birds of the sea-shore had never before been reported to me, I started the next afternoon, hindered and baffled by a strong and bitter wind which soon turned to pelting rain, and by a toothache which raged in sympathy with the elements; but I was rewarded for my pains. I found the Dunlins; but I found also what was far more wonderful and beautiful – the whole length of the river's bank, on the meadow side of it, occupied by countless Yellow Wagtails. As I walked along they got up literally from under my feet; for they were sheltering just beneath the meadow's lip, and I came upon them quite unawares. When a turn in the bank gave me a view ahead, I could see the turf spotted all over with the brilliant yellow of their breasts; for I was walking with the wind, and they, of course, were facing it, to avoid having their plumage uncomfortably handled by the gusts.

They were not afraid of me, and settled down again, directly I had passed on, so that my progress was like that of a haymaking machine, which just lifts the hay as it passes, and then lets it settle down again after dallying a moment with the breeze. These birds had clearly only just arrived after their long journey from Africa, and I think they must have come together and unpaired; the greater number of them were males. Their numbers diminished regularly day by day, and at the same time I began to see pairs in their usual places in the neighbourhood evidently preparing to nest. In a few days they were nearly all distributed over the country-side.

Since then I have looked out for them every year and have always seen plenty in mid-April on this same meadow, but never again such a wonderful assemblage. The nearest approach to it was on 22nd April of this present year, 1894. I had walked some miles up the river without seeing a single Wagtail, and had made up my mind that they had not yet come, when, as I was returning home across the Port Meadow, my dog ran into a bevy of them, and sent them dancing into the air, uttering their bright shrill whistle. As before, they soon settled down again; and now I noticed how hard it was to see them on the ground. Their greenish-brown backs assimilated admirably with the freshly-grown grass, and their breasts were hardly to be distinguished from the marigolds among which they had settled.

Of the nesting of the Yellow Wagtail among these marigolds and buttercups I can say nothing from personal experience. I have never found the nest, and it is so well concealed as to have baffled the most indefatigable nest-finder I know. The birds are so restless, and so happily artful in misleading you, that even if you know within twenty yards or so where the nest must be, the task of finding it needs more time and patience than most of us have to spare.

But though it thus hides its nest and eggs with infinite care, it is astonishing how bold this little bird will be in the breeding time; more than once it has let me approach it within a yard or two as it runs delicately through the grass, picking off invisible insects from the fresh shoots; and several times I have known it decoy both me and my dog away from the nest, by letting us come very close, and then running or half flying a little way on in front. It knows very well that a dog is dangerous; and I once saw both cock and hen stand up to Billy in such a ludicrously determined way, – the cock in front as if to protect his wife – that I stopped the dog with a sign, and the big and little animals continued to regard each other on equal terms, until my irrepressible laughter sent the Wagtails off.

When the young are able to fly, I know no more beautiful sight than to watch them playing in a hayfield. True, they are not of the bright yellow their parents wear, – they are often almost wholly brown, though they differ considerably from each other; but their movements in the air it is a constant pleasure to watch. They dance and spring and twist and turn, – now they are on the ground, now high in air, now at the other end of the field, and now as suddenly back again. Nor do they limit themselves to the hay-fields, or to the pastures where they run about among the legs of the grazing cattle. I have repeatedly seen them in osier-beds, on telegraph wires, on the top branches of high trees, and in cornfields perching on the ears of wheat. So light and sylph-like are they that the stalks were hardly bent beneath their weight; and I could not help singling out one of these on which a bird had been resting, and trying to measure with the touch of my finger the weight of that fairy figure. Another day I watched a family perched upon the telegraph wires; they let me come close underneath them, and now and then performed the feat of running sideways along the wires, holding on chiefly by means of the hind claw, which is very long. This claw was brought round below the wire to join the others, and thus around each wire a complete little ring was formed, which seemed to slide along it when the birds moved.

The tail of this bird is not so long in proportion as in the two other Wagtails, nor is it moved so frequently or regularly. As he runs about among the cows you will see very little 'wagging' going on – hardly more than in the common Meadow-pipit. But no sooner does he take to flight than his tail becomes the most conspicuous part of him; it seems to twist and open, showing clearly the pure white outer feathers, and when he once more alights, it will be vibrated two or three times. Then the movement ceases, and the white is hardly to be seen.

The mention of tails brings me naturally to the last and the most beautiful of our three species, the so-called Grey Wagtail of the running streams; for in his case the tail is not only the most prominent feature, as it is in all Wagtails, but is longer than in the rest, and in much more constant motion. Here there are no ornithological puzzles to detain us. It seems that you may roam over the whole continents of Europe and Asia, and see the same bird that haunts our own mountain streams.

Every fisherman knows the Grey Wagtail and will bear me out when I say once more that grey is not quite the word for him. If he stands facing you as you fish up-stream, he will show you his black gorget of the breeding season, and the beautiful yellow of his under parts; or if you chance to see him from behind, though his head and back will show slate-grey, yet this as it nears the tail becomes greenish-yellow, and the tail itself is not grey but nearly black in colour, with the two outer feathers bright white. The bird is in fact at a first glance not unlike the Yellow Wagtail, with which it has often been confused; but the black gorget brings it rather into relation with the Pied Wagtail, which has the same conspicuous addition to its dress in spring. Yet from both birds it is quite distinct, in habits as well as appearance, and seems to stand entirely by itself in the little world of Wagtails.

In this island it is always resident; but here, and apparently in all countries where it dwells, it desires a change of scene, and perhaps of food, in autumn. In the lower and flatter lands it is rarely seen in spring and summer: in Oxfordshire it seldom fails to appear in September or even earlier, and as regularly leaves us in January or February. Now and again a pair will stay to breed by some lock or mill-dam, where they find the constant rush of water which they so dearly love.

I have once known this bird build at some little distance from tumbling water, and in a position where I should never have thought of looking for the nest. I was strolling before breakfast in the garden of the Hotel Titlis at Engelberg, in which there is a small ornamental water, with a boat and boathouse. Standing on a bridge which crossed this water, I watched a Grey Wagtail with food in its bill which was hovering about the entrance of this boathouse. At last it went in, and, following it, I found the nest on the timber shelf from which the roof sprang. Later on, with the help of a friend's lusty shoulders, I managed to get a look into it; it was large and untidy, like the Pied Wagtail's nest in the greenhouse, or like those of the Spotted Flycatcher.

So long as the young broods are unable wholly to shift for themselves, they seem to keep together under the eye of the parents, and will play together like Wagtails of other kinds. On 26th June 1887 I was strolling on a mountain path in the Bernese Oberland, and came suddenly into a little glen, down which a stream rushed babbling, at the foot of a wall of rock some fifty feet high. Dancing about stream and rock, like black and yellow fairies, and occasionally resting on the rock's face, or on the young pines which grew about it, was a family, or perhaps two families, of these most graceful birds. So restless were they, so quick and nimble that the eye could hardly follow them and it was with the greatest difficulty that I got my glass fixed on one of them. The same agility is shown when they come down in September from the mountains, which are then getting too cool for them, and congregate by the banks of some large river in a valley. I have seen them in great numbers just after their arrival, very busy in catching flies over the water of a rushing glacier-stream, and mixing with their cousins the White Wagtails;

the air was full of dancing birds, and the banks alive with gently-moving tails. As they hung in air over the stream, the tail was often spread out wide, like that of a hovering Kestrel, while the rapidly-moving wings danced them up and down.

But as a rule, when grown older, the Grey Wagtails are somewhat quiet and deliberate in their ways, though always full of grace; they are, if I may use the word of both sexes, extremely ladylike birds. And there is a look in them of great content, and even of self-satisfaction, as they trip along, unaware that they are observed, by the water's edge; with no lack of food, with the pleasant noise of the water ever in their ears, and with those long tails of theirs perpetually moving up and down, as if in rhythm with the water. It is worth noting that the motion of these tails is not exactly that which we have observed in the other two species; it is not so purely a tail-motion, and it is less rapid and more regular. It is a motion of the whole body from the breast tailwards; it is only the great length of the feathers that gives it the appearance of belonging to the tail only. The verb to *wag* is utterly inapplicable to it, nor can I think of any word which will exactly express it. One other bird that haunts our British streams has the very same movement of the whole body, and this is one which has but little tail – the Common Sandpiper.

Before I leave these tails I have yet a few words to say about them. In this scientific age when questions beginning with *why* are always being asked, if seldom finally answered, I might feel it a duty to the Wagtails to ask the reason of their tail-motions. I do not indeed promise to explain them, not – at least with the easy conviction of a certain popular writer, who (though it is but lately that he learnt the difference between the Grey and the Yellow Wagtails) assures us boldly that the object of the motion is to aid the bird in balancing itself. It is true enough, no doubt, that the tail of every bird is of use to it in this way, especially in the air; but the peculiar motion of the tails I am writing of cannot possibly be needed for this purpose. If the birds were likely to topple over into the water while sitting on the edge of a stone

– a supposition in itself absurd, – I imagine that it would most naturally keep its tail well down rather than wave it up and down rapidly. But surely no bird needs any peculiar action to enable it to keep its equipoise; even a sparrow without a tail can do this perfectly well. Again, if the Wagtails need long tails and a peculiar motion to keep them steady, how does the Dipper manage – a bird that needs balancing on slippery stones as much at least as they? His tail is short, his form less shapely than that of a Wagtail, and as he sits on the edge of a stone making bows at you, he takes no such precautions to save himself from a tumble as in his ignorance of a bird's make and habits this writer attributes to the Wagtails.

For several years I have closely observed the tail-motions, not only of Wagtails, but of a great variety of birds, and I may fairly venture to express an opinion about them. It is a familiar fact that many animals use their tails to express certain emotions; for the tail is directly connected with the spinal cord and the brain, and may become an index or reflector of what is going on within that brain. Tails may of course be used in different ways; the cat waves its tail when it is angry, the dog when it is pleased. That is merely matter of habit; but in each case the motion is the result of some affection of the nervous system. Now the nervous system of birds is very sensitive, if we may judge by their restlessness, and by the extreme vigilance and rapidity of their sight and all their motions. And this in many birds, and especially in small ones, is apt to show itself in the tail, which is flickered horizontally as in the Redstart, or jerked upwards, as in the Wren and Moorhen, or twitched several times in a minute, as in the Yellowhammer and Reed Bunting, the Wheatear and Whinchat, and others. The motion may mean either simple satisfaction, or sometimes distress and alarm. With most of the birds I have mentioned the former is the cause, though not, I think, invariably; but watch a Red-backed Shrike as you approach his nest or young, and you will see a good example of the effect of anger on a tail. He sits on the top of the hedge, swinging his tail from side to side, as well as up and down, with a motion quite peculiar to himself, and uttering cries that make the meaning of the motion unmistakable.

The tail-motions of the Wagtails, if I am not mistaken, is no great mystery; it is no more than a nervous trick, which in their case, as in that of so many others, expresses happiness and satisfaction. The Pied Wagtail which I watched on the lawn half an hour ago showed me this as plainly as possible. When he first alighted on the lawn he 'wagged' his tail, and every time he caught an insect he did so. The Grey Wagtail, a quieter bird, as we have seen, has developed a habit of constant motion which is, indeed, second nature with him, and as plainly speaks his content with his surroundings as does the flicker of the Redstart in the orchard.

But we are not yet quite at the end of the matter. Every one who has noticed these tail-motions at all must have been struck by their constant correlation with those white feathers which are so conspicuous in the Wagtails. And the Wagtails are by no means alone in this peculiarity; for it is astonishing how many European birds show white either in their tails or tail-coverts, and how large a number of these have some nervous trick which makes this white conspicuous. The Moorhen is a good example. I have seen her leading her young brood across the water, jerking her tail so that its white is constantly visible to them, and at the same time calling them to follow the standard they see thus held out for them. I have seen an old Reed Bunting sitting on a rail and calling his young about him, while at every twitch of his tail it was just so much expanded as to show the white, and with the white his position. I believe, then, that in these and some other instances the nervous trick has a secondary use; it is not only a sign of satisfaction, but also a signal, and the white *a recognition mark.*

Bindon Hill

The innumerable rabbits which burrow on the hillside

I often doubt whether there can be such another hill as Bindon in these islands; I at least have never found it. In foreign lands there are famous hills, and health-giving hills – Alesia, Epipolai, or the Acropolis; but I feel sure that they cannot offer such store of delights, for mind and body too, as Bindon does. Tropical hills may be gorgeous and overpowering, but they are often, to say the least of it, uncomfortable. Under the shadow of Bindon I am just now reading Darwin's *Voyage Round the World*, and have been crossing the Andes with him, and trying to penetrate by perilous paths into the mountainous recesses of Tahiti. I have been led to fancy that if the *Beagle* could but have sailed into the little cove that lies under Bindon's flank, as into a newly-discovered harbour, and have landed the great naturalist to take a walk and explore the overhanging down, he would have carried away such recollections of insects, plants, birds, views, geological strata, and fresh air, as would have made his usually sedate page eloquent of pleasure never to be forgotten.

Those who now sail, or rather steam, into this deep and tranquil cove are in the summer season to be numbered by thousands. They come from all the watering-places near at hand, they come and eat and stroll and depart, and, fortunately for me, they rarely discover Bindon. For Bindon rears his crest some five hundred and fifty feet above the sea at his base, and is not very easy of access from the steamers' landing-place. I do not think that I myself truly discovered him the first time I came here, even under the tuition of a valued friend who had known him from boyhood; I trod his whole length more than once, but my diary shows me that I did not understand him. For ten successive years I have never once missed him altogether; and now when his well-known form comes in sight from the window of the train, I feel youth still stirring in me with strong desire to mount upon his grassy back.

I cannot paint Bindon, and indeed I think he does not readily suggest beauties to the artist's eye. I have twice walked his whole length in company with a young artist, who saw nothing on either occasion to delay him. Turner has drawn the steep cliffs with which his western end strikes down into the cove, but they are not the chief objects in the drawing, nor do they give you any idea of what Bindon really is. The magnificent precipice of his eastern end, pure white chalk falling sheer into a clear blue sea, was the subject of a picture in a water-colour exhibition not long ago. But, except at his two extremities, Bindon is not attractive to artists; and to understand him truly it is not enough to contemplate him from without. You must spend whole mornings with him, lying on him, and *being of him*. Better to be bookless there, in my opinion, even on the warmest day; I cannot keep my attention on the page, there is so much life and fragrance around me. There is so much that is beautiful to look at, not for the artist, but for me; whether I turn southward to the sparkling sea with its white sails, or look northward over long miles of a purple heathery plain, or lie down and look into the long dry grass which the sun is turning golden, and catch the millions of gossamer webs, stretched by some invisible fairy spider from blade to blade over the sward.

But we will contemplate Bindon for a moment, and stoop to consider him outwardly as a hill, before we stretch ourselves upon his back and see what he has to show us. He is nothing more than a mighty mound of chalk, nearly two miles long, and rising to his highest point about midway; yet he is unlike any other chalk hill I know of along the whole southern coast. He has an individuality quite his own, and all the creatures seem to know and love it. Even among the hills of his own narrow range – a range full twenty miles in length – Bindon is quite unique in the charm he exercises over all bees, butterflies and grasshoppers.

This curious individuality of his is easily understood if he be looked at in front, either from the sea or inland from the north, so that his whole length is seen at once, together with the long ridge of which he really forms a part, stretching far to east and west. In all this range Bindon is the only isolated hill; he does not slide easily down to any saddle which connects him too familiarly with another rise; he stands alone, and the sea washes his base at either end. As you approach him from the east along the ridge, you become aware that you must descend into a gap to the sea-level, and then toil upwards for nearly a mile before you reach his highest point. And when you stand at last on the top, you find that you have yet nearly another mile before you drop down at his western end to the shore of the little cove I spoke of. Thus Bindon demands his tribute of those who would worship on his high places; but he is a hospitable and kindly hill, generous to all who know him. At the very first step you take in mounting him from Arishmill Gap he offers you, even in the most arid season, a draught of clear cold water, bubbling up ready filtered from beneath his deep chalky recesses; he has prepared for you a smooth track of soft elastic sward, which carries you up till all your real labour is over; and then, when you are getting hot and tired, he has ready for you without fail a cool breeze – a breeze like a happy conversation with a friend you prize, in which you can lie down in solitude and yet not be alone. This is so on most days from May till October; on every day, that is, which you would naturally choose for a walk along these noble hills.

Bindon's individuality, then, is chiefly to be explained by his isolation, and I am much inclined to think that the animal life in which he abounds is in a measure isolated too. And this is made all the more likely, as I fancy, by the fact that Bindon has a lowland territory which is all his own, quite distinct from his turfy uplands. Within his mighty embrace, on the side towards the sea, there lies at his feet a space of land a mile long, and in its broadest part a third of a mile wide, which is completely shut in by the sea beyond it, by the precipitous cliffs of Bindon's two extremities, and by his own steep slopes rising from the whole length of it to the northward. It is cultivated, but carelessly; for it is naturally exposed to the salt breezes, and the farmer to whom it belongs can only reach it by a rough chalky track which crosses Bindon at an angle like a pipeclayed shoulder-belt. His great waggons cannot be taken over this, but you may meet a rude cart laden with some thin-looking produce jolting slowly down the ruts towards the farm, and looking as though at any moment it might send its burden rolling down the grassy steep. This curious tract of half-wild land is thus in reality a part of Bindon; but its vegetation is totally different from his. Here, and on the rocks and broken sandy slopes which overlook the sea, grow many curious plants, as well as abundance of thistles and other ordinary weeds; and here, I think, the butterflies, which so abound in the summer on Bindon's back and flanks, must pass the earlier stages of their existence as caterpillars and chrysalides, until their wings enable them to seek for change of scene and fresh blossoms on the heights above.

The geological relation of Bindon to this lower territory of his is an interesting one; and, though no geologist, I may venture a word on what addresses itself so readily to an eye

at all accustomed to observe. Bindon is a single segment in a
long spine of chalk down stretching from Weymouth Bay to
Poole Harbour. The whole of this spine was at one time
protected from the sea by a rampart of Portland rock, with
which it was connected by a series of beds of sand and clay.
In its eastern half it is still so protected; from Swanage Bay to
Arishmill Gap the voracious sea has never been able to set
his mark upon it. But the little stream that at this latter point
makes its way to the sea – the only one that pierces the range
during its entire length – has here eaten away the chalky
strata in the course of ages; and here too the fronting
rampart has given way to the sea, leaving only a few jagged
rocks, well loved of cormorants, to show where it once stood.
In came the remorseless tide, washing away the intervening
clay and sand, till it reached Bindon's eastern flank, where
sea and weather between them at last exposed those
magnificent white cliffs. At his western end too the sea has
found an entrance, and, breaking through the rampart here
again, has wrought out a beautiful circular basin by the
regular wash of its tides; here again, too, making raids on
Bindon's western end, where even now the traces are plain of
dangerous falls of chalk, one of which (so the coastguards-
man tells me) raised last winter a roar like that of an
avalanche. But in front of the whole length of Bindon, from
the cove to the eastern cliffs, the protecting rampart still
stands firm; the sea has found no chance to eat away the
clayey and sandy strata which lie between this bulwark and
the chalk; and it is here that they still form that tract of
half-wild land which Bindon may claim as his own territory,
enclosed as it is between his two precipitous ends, his steep
southern front and the sea.

If this description has been at all comprehensible, it will
perhaps occur to the reader that Bindon must offer a
splendid position to an enemy landing on the coast, or to
a tribe driven from the interior and clinging to the last
available defence. The low-lying land that he shuts in would
supply both food and water; sheep could pasture on his
summit; and the exceeding steepness of his sides would make

it impossible, without artillery, to carry the hill in the face of
a sufficient number of defenders. And that Bindon has at one
time been put to some such use as this there is very clear
evidence to be found. At the top of the steepest part of the
entire length of his landward front there runs a well-marked
double line of fortification; not indeed such huge trenches
and ramparts as once made an impregnable fortress of
Maiden Castle near Dorchester, or even such as guarded
Ring Hill, Bindon's nearest neighbour to the eastward, but a
line which was once no doubt, quite sufficient for its purpose,
touching the precipitous cliffs at each extremity of the hill,
and strengthened at the western end, where the slope is
rather less steep than elsewhere, by an inner line of defence
much stronger than the outer one.

What people made these fortifications, in what age, and
with what object? I have hunted in massive books of
antiquities for answers to these questions, but their splendid
quarto pages speak, as usual, with a most uncertain sound.
How, indeed, should any one have an answer, or one that is
not wildest guesswork? Did some invading chieftain steer his
black ships into the cove, and possess himself of Bindon, as a
first step to the conquest of the inland country? Or was this
the refuge of the people of the district round about, to which
they could fly at the approach of an enemy from the north?
There is a sense of melancholy in these blind attempts to
pierce the utterly forgotten past; all the human endeavour,
endurance, and courage that may have spent itself on Bindon
has vanished for ever, leaving only these dumb earthworks
to tempt the local antiquary into fanciful conjecture.

But these are mere accidents of Bindon; slight human
scratchings on his massive form. Let us climb up on his back,
and see what he himself really is, – how he clothes himself,
and what creatures delight to live on him and about him.

The monster's shaggy hide is, perhaps, the first of his real
attributes that seizes on the eye. Each steep flank is clothed
with this hide; it is now, in autumn following a dry summer,
brown and withered, but not mangy-looking like that which
some of his neighbours wear. In the summer it is a soft

golden-green, which the sun looks into lovingly and lights up, for the ends and edges of the longer blades are always brown, which passes into a golden glow as the sun comes from behind a cloud. On the steep slopes it hangs downwards just like a living creature's fell; and I believe it has been this, more than anything else about him, which has always made me think of Bindon as a huge reposing animal. This grass has one quality which is most delightful to those who have learnt to know Bindon well. It is at all times so thirsty that it absorbs moisture with most astonishing rapidity; on the southern and more sunny side the rain or sea-mist is at once drawn into the chalky soil, but on the northern, where the grass is thicker and longer, if you probe with your fingers you may feel a touch of dampness in a mossy undergrowth. But there is no need to be alarmed at this; the hide protects you from it like a waterproof and you may cast yourself down on it half an hour after a shower, if the sun be shining, without a thought of rheumatism.

On Bindon's narrow spine, – and it is another peculiarity of his, which I have not mentioned, that he narrows towards his highest point, till the ridge itself is not more than a dozen paces across, – on this narrow spine of his, and on many a level spot elsewhere, there grows a short and velvety turf, as deliciously elastic to the tread as the air that breathes over it is exhilarating to the mind. Touch it with a stick, and it will in some places give gently to the pressure; and if you cut out a bit with a penknife, you find a depth of an inch or more of a soft, black, peaty substance. It is here that on a summer evening you may see the green lamp of the glow-worm, even at this height of five hundred feet; striped shells of all colours are strewn about here, chiefly the endless varieties of one abundant species. Spiders and beetles are to be sought for rather in the fringe of longer grass which bounds these turfy spaces; but the chirruping grasshopper is everywhere. At every step this September they leap out by twos and threes; and I think it must be these which are just now attracting such numbers of Kestrels to Bindon's southern slopes, where the life in the grass is most abundant. They are hovering all

around, not high in the air, as one sees them inland, or
waiting long on motionless wing till you are tired of watching
them, but poising themselves for a minute not many yards
above the grass, and then quietly settling down on it to eat
their prey. So intent are they on this pursuit, that you may
occasionally creep quite close to them, though not quite
close enough to see what it is they are after. No one seems to
molest these beautiful birds; the folk here, by calling them
'Beetle-hawks,' show plainly that they associate them with
no mischief to the innumerable rabbits which burrow on the
hillside; and indeed, if they did now and then carry off a
young one, more good would perhaps be done than harm.
So they are left to enjoy on Bindon a paradise of peace
and plenty, very different from the lot of our hard-driven
Kestrels of the too-well-preserved midlands.

In the summer the air of Bindon is sweet with thyme; but
it is in September that I have most often been here, when the
wealth of bloom is over. There are, indeed, still plenty of
flowers, all of them blue, purple, or yellow, and nearly all
small in size. The plants are here all dwarfed, like those of
the high Alps; they nestle down in the soft herbage, not
caring to put out long stalks which might be rudely handled
by strong winds. Among these is one which in September is
Bindon's special ornament, peering up with an upright
corolla of deep purple wherever the grass is short; some
plants are bolder than the others, and shoot up for three or
four inches, branching into a little cluster, while often you
see but one purple bell, the base of which is quite hidden in
the turf. This is a campanula which grows to some height in
the hedgerows below; but it is apt in richer soil to become a
somewhat coarse and untidy plant, and never equals in
beauty the little gentian-like bell-flower of the hills.

Hovering over these plants and over harebell, hawkweed,
scabious, and dwarf thistle, are innumerable humble-bees
and butterflies. Even at the very top, and on a breezy day, a
Red Admiral will pass you, fresh from the chrysalis, with
that matchless flight of his. The Painted Lady is almost as
beautiful, and this year she is to be seen everywhere here; the

more sober-coloured Grayling too is always abundant on Bindon. The Clouded Yellow is to be found here in most years, and is now in extraordinary numbers; I have seen also a single specimen of the beautiful pale variety. The Marbled White affects one end of Bindon, and the exquisite Clifden Blue the other; the latter haunting the warm sunny hollows on the southern side, where its delicate wings do not get caught too roughly by the wind. The Chalk Hill Blue and the Common Blue are to be seen on most chalk downs, and they are in great abundance here; but the bright sheen of the wings of the Clifden Blue is a thing to be remembered, and it is not too often seen.

At the base of Bindon is one of the few homes of a Skipper peculiar to this stretch of coast – a sober-coloured little butterfly, which still survives the raids made upon it by collectors. And as the Skippers bring us by an easy transition to the moths, I will mention a strange spectacle I once came upon, and have never chanced to see again. Almost at the very top of the hill, in the little hollow of the fortifying lines, there were thistles growing to about a foot in height, and all of them in bloom; on each flower there were from two to six handsome Burnet-moths, and at the base of each plant lay the dead bodies of others! I must have walked two hundred yards at least before I left the thistles and their crowded occupants behind me.

But after all it is the bird-life on Bindon which gives me the greatest pleasure. Beside the Kestrels, whose way of living is altogether gentle and harmless, the fiercer Sparrowhawk is to be seen here; a far more dangerous bird, both for the young rabbit and for the conspicuous Wheatear, whose bright white patch on the upper tail-coverts marks him out as an easy prey. I was once just reaching the crest of the down two or three miles to the westward, and had my eye on a Wheatear who was flicking his tail and bowing after his manner on a stone hard by, when a Sparrowhawk suddenly shot over the ridge in front of me, swooped upon the bird, missed his aim, tumbled right over on the ground, and then seeing me went off, doubtless in a bad temper. Now and then a still more formidable bird of prey will sail over Bindon. Only the other day he passed over me as I lay on the grass; sweeping upwards to the white cliffs, he sent the little birds flying in all directions, then turned, – whether with a victim in his claws I could not see, – and in a moment, as it seemed, was full a mile away. This is the Peregrine Falcon, who still

On each flower there were handsome burnet moths

holds his own, and has somewhere every year a nest among these abrupt cliffs. And but half an hour ago a Raven passed along the entire length of Bindon in little more than a minute, – a rare sight, though once in April I have seen and heard a pair circling round the inaccessible cliff not far away to westward, where that year they must have built their nest.

The Gulls, of course, are Bindon's especial pride; but just now they are nearly all from home, gone inland perhaps to feed on the newly-ploughed fields. Only when the schools of mackerel have come into the bay, darkening and making crisp the water here and there beneath the cliffs where Gulls and Cormorants breed together in spring, have we seen a Herring-gull arrive mysteriously and suddenly, hover over the disturbed water for a moment while catching the whitebait which the mackerel are chasing, and then settle down quietly on the wave to swallow and digest. No other sea-bird seemed to follow these shoals; but the fishermen were waiting for them with a huge net, and twice we were there to see a great draught of fishes – more than a thousand mackerel twinkling with prismatic hues in the sunlight, tiny whitebait suffering the same fate, as their enemies, with here and there a plaice, a sole, a prickly John Dory, a whiting, or a heavy, leathery-mouthed 'sea-carp'.

Of the other birds of Bindon I have hardly space to tell; of the cheerful Titlarks which abound on the summit, and sometimes descend to the shore to join their cousins the Rock-Pipits, and to enjoy a change of diet; of the House-martins, which are here Rock-martins, building their nests under the ledges of Bindon's eastern cliffs; of the Stock-doves, whose splendid deep-blue plumage one can often admire here from above – a thing impossible in the flat country. I must pass by the Stonechats that abound on the hedges below, and the Ring-ousels that every autumn rest here awhile on migration, betraying themselves by their loud, metallic alarm-note, and, if they happen to face you, as indeed they rarely do, by the conspicuous white crescent on their breasts. Even my favourites, the Wagtails, must be no more than mentioned; all the three common species have shown themselves to me on Bindon's slopes, or by the spring at his foot, during the last few days, all probably travelling quietly eastward.

But of the great stream of migration that can be watched in mid-September from the top of Bindon I must needs say just a word. If the wind be blowing gently from east or north, so that the travellers do not have it directly behind them, take a station anywhere on the narrow ridge, and look for the passage of Swallows and Martins from west to east. They will come in parties great or small, and if the day is warm and the breeze on their beam, they will dally a while on Bindon's flanks, and may deceive you into fancying that they are his own birds. But watch steadily, and you will see that they are gradually passing you; follow them with the glass to the eastward, and you may make sure that they are hastening to some point where the Channel is narrower and where perhaps they will wait a day or two for a favourable crossing. Rarely do they travel with a strong wind behind them; it carries them too fast to allow them to collect food, and disturbs the sit of their feathers. Once I have seen a few in this predicament, and travelling so straight and so swiftly that I tried to time them with the seconds-hand of my watch. To the best of my belief they covered half a mile in fifteen seconds, or little more; they were therefore making nearly two miles in a minute, and supposing they went straight on at the same pace, might reach the coast of Kent in little more than an hour.

But they will not go so far tonight; the sun is sinking, and, clear as all the country is to the northward, there is a mist rising from the sea which will presently wrap Bindon in its soft and moist embrace.

Let us take one last look before we descend; first at the grey and misty sea, then by St. Aldhelm's Head and Ballard down by Swanage to Poole Harbour and the little ancient town of Wareham, at the eastern end of that great heath of which the Dorsetshire novelist has told more than one sad tale; and so northward along the distant line of those 'crowns o' D'set downs' of which the Dorsetshire poet has sung in his tender mood and quaint language, till the eye reaches in the west the monument to Nelson's Hardy, and Weymouth Bay and Portland, where on the Bill the two warning lights will soon begin to twinkle. And lastly, as the russet and lavender tints of autumn twilight begin to spread over the hills nearer at hand, it is pleasant to let the eye drop upon that little village nestling in the deep curve of the valley below us – our home at night as Bindon is our home by day, from whose dark red chimneys 'azure pillars of the hearth' arise to mingle with the growing twilight.

Even now it is hard to leave Bindon; but he is composing himself to sleep with all the life that is about him – unless indeed those fairy spiders spin their gossamer in the stillness of the night, to adorn him in the morning's sunlight with a network of intangible lace.

Departing Birds

We crossed the harbour in a boat

The last days of summer slip away only too quickly, and the birds slip away with them, often quite unobserved. It is much easier to record the arrival of birds accurately than their departure. They themselves are more active, and many of them are more showy, when they come in spring; they perform their journey more rapidly, and are obviously eager to reach their old summer homes. We too are apt to be more alert at that time; the few dead weeks of February and early March are followed by a season when all who live in the country with their eyes open are daily in that state of good spirits which realised expectations bring with them. But when the last comer among the birds has brought up his young, when the songs have ceased and the moulting has begun, it may be that we fall in with the humour of the birds and become less active and less keenly observant. However that may be – and I have no right to speak but for myself – it is at least true that any given observer will have less to tell you of the dates of departure than of the dates of the arrival of birds in his district.

There are several reasons for this besides the want of

continuous patient observation. During the moult the birds are apt to disappear from view, and when it is over, unless they begin to sing again – which they will not do in unfavourable weather – we may easily miss them or fancy that they have altogether deserted us. Then comes another difficulty. Our own local birds may really have left us, and yet we may be deceived into thinking that they are still here by the appearance of individuals of the same species, which are in reality only resting for a day or two in the course of their leisurely travel. For example, I should find it hard to say with any certainty at what time the Whinchats leave my own neighbourhood, though the bird is very abundant and obvious here all through the summer. I can state without hesitation that they were with us till the end of August; on the 26th of that month they were in large numbers about their favourite nesting-places on the railway banks. I was away the greater part of September, and today (1st October) I am unable to find a single Whinchat. But I should not be surprised if I were to see one or two more; they have occasionally been here as late as this. Should they appear again I shall conclude that these are travellers from the north and west, and that our own birds made their start during my absence in September.

Something may be done by keeping a daily list of all birds seen during August and September; in this way not only will the last appearance of some residents be detected, but a few casual travellers may fall into the net. Something too may be done by following the migrants on their journey, making up the list of all birds seen, as at home. Unfortunately it is not possible to be at home and to travel at the same time; and ornithologists are usually attracted in the autumn by the vast *immigration* of birds into this country from the east and north, and find much more interesting occupation on our eastern coast than on the western or southern districts. This year I stayed at home till 4th September, keeping a list in conjunction with two nephews, boys who were being initiated into the mysteries of ornithology as an agreeable holiday task. From the 12th to the 26th of September I travelled with one of them in the south of England, beginning in Cornwall and finishing in Kent. In neither period were the results at all striking, nor indeed did I expect that they would be; but, taken in conjunction with the observations of other years, they may be worth setting down.

During the whole of the three weeks in August which we spent here at Kingham, we were continually walking or driving about the country, and I doubt if we could well have missed any birds which were about; I was aided by two pairs of sharp young eyes and ears, and was called upon to look at and identify almost every bird that showed himself. Yet it is a singular fact that until the very last day we failed to bring the Skylark into our list. It could hardly have been the case that the Larks were all skulking in the standing corn, for it was being cut all round us in the latter half of August. There were plenty of Skylarks breeding here in the summer, and there are plenty here now – the first day of October. If their absence in August is to be explained on the ground that they were hiding during the moult, it is at least odd that not a single one should have met our eyes during three weeks. I am almost tempted to guess that our own Larks had left the neighbourhood, possibly to migrate by the south coast to the continent, and that the birds we have with us now are arrivals from the east and north. But such a conjecture can have no value unless it be supported by a long series of observations; and much may doubtless be urged against it.

Another familiar bird was also wholly missing – the Corn Bunting. Ours is a district in which this bird delights, and I was under the impression that I could produce one for inspection at any time of year. But whether they were skulking and moulting, – in an even more melancholy state of mind than usual, – or whether they had really left us, it is certain that they were not to be found. The Corn Bunting is not celebrated as a migrant; but it is well known to ornithologists that its numbers are largely increased in the autumn by arrivals from the north of Europe, and it is possible that in this case too our resident birds had already left us to make room for the new-comers.

These were our most notable absentees. All our regular summer visitors were with us, though perhaps in diminishing numbers, except the Cuckoo, the Nightingale (which disappears mysteriously, I know not when), and the Swifts and Shrikes, the last birds to arrive in May. These last left us while we were forming our list. On 16th August it was pretty plain that the Swifts were going and that the summer was drawing to an end. We saw one or two on the 18th and 19th, and on the 27th, a small party passed on migration. This was the last we saw of them. In 1891, the year in which the whole tribe of Swallows and Martins was so late in leaving us, the last Swifts were seen here on the fourth of September; and I have seen them even later on the coast of Dorset. The Red-backed Shrikes had left their nesting-places at the end of July, and I did not see another till 26th August, when a young bird, which most probably had missed his way on his travels, appeared on the telegraph wires, and was gone the next day.

Other stray travellers began to show themselves as August crept on, and made up for the comparative dullness of that month for the ornithologist. Not indeed that most beautiful bird the Green Sandpiper which for years used to enliven our Augusts; he has deserted us for some inscrutable reason, and left his favourite stream to the Kingfishers, which are now again growing more abundant every year. But a fine show of orange-red berries of the mountain ash in my garden brought a new and strange visitor, for whose sake, would he but have stayed, I would willingly have sacrificed them. The thrush tribe are so passionately fond of these berries that I enjoy the sight of them for only a very few days; and this year a young Ring-ousel, the only one I have ever seen in the neighbourhood, having no doubt lost his way on migration, found these out and hankered after them for a whole day. He startled me by his unmistakable alarm note early in the morning of 16th August, and again and again that day he tried to get at the berries flying round and round while we were playing on the lawn, and in spite of his natural wildness alighting now and then on the tree, but always on the side of it away from us. But even such hard won luxuries could not detain him long; he was gone next morning.

We cannot be in the line of the Ring-ousel's travel for the only other occurrence of which I have a record is that of a wanderer who was killed against the telegraph wires many years ago. I rather think that in coming from the north they prefer the high ground, and take the line of the Cotswolds, where I found them on the 1st September of last year, and so pass over the Wiltshire downs to the south coast; while the Welsh birds collect in suitable cover on the south coast of Wales, where I have often seen them in autumn, and cross to Exmoor over the Bristol Channel. But the Wheatears which rarely or never breed about here, regularly take us in their autumn migration, and in much larger numbers than we see in the spring. This year the first appeared on 24th August, dotted about in certain favourite fields; and then for several days they were to be found together with the Whinchats on the railway banks and telegraph wires.

Meanwhile the Swallows and Martins had begun to collect on sunny mornings on the roof of my house, and a vast gathering of them in a neighbouring village warned us that migration was at hand. On 14th September I left for Falmouth, hoping to see something of what these birds were doing in the far west, and to follow them eastwards if they had begun to move. But here the weather, which had been very cold and rainy, suddenly changed, and we came again into a summer which was tempting the birds to linger. The morning after our arrival we crossed the harbour in a boat to a beautiful sunny promontory, with wood and gorse coming down to the water; it was positively hot, and birds and butterflies were abundant. In the gorse at one warm spot my nephew caught a sound which I should have missed if I had been alone; he wished to know what it was, and, pushing a little way into the gorse, I heard to my astonishment the reel of the Grasshopper Warbler. It was new to me that this bird ever finds his voice again in the autumn.

In a day or two the fine weather showed signs of breaking

up, and the birds began to move a little. Along the beach the
Pied Wagtails were dallying, yet clearly moving eastwards,
and among them were one or two unmistakable White
Wagtails.– birds which we do not often see in Oxfordshire.
One of these was a very conspicuous adult bird, with the
black crescent in front remarkably bright and the upper
parts a uniform light grey – so light in fact that the bird
seemed almost white as he flitted past me. A journey to St.
Ives on the western coast, showed us a very large collection
of Wagtails on the fields above the beach, and among these
too there seemed to be one or two of the rarer species. The
Pied Wagtail, the Meadow Pipit, and the Linnet – of which
last there were in some places immense numbers – were the
three species which obliged us with their companionship
during the whole of our travel along the south coast.

It was only on the last day of our stay at Falmouth that the
Swallows and Martins began to show distinct signs of
migration. That day they were passing in small parties over
the promontory where we had found the Grasshopper
Warbler, all going pretty steadily eastwards. Next day, the
19th, I saw from the train window just east of Exeter a vast
congregation of them, extending at least two or three miles.
This leads me to suspect that the birds which pass along the
north coast of Somerset and Devon, coming from Wales and
the Severn valley, cross the latter county to the south by way
of Barnstaple and the river Taw, and then, instead of
striking the sea at Exmouth, follow an inland route eastwards, past Honiton and Axminster, until they reach the
Dorset coast. By the sea at Sidmouth, where we spent one
whole day, we saw nothing of them; that loveliest of
watering-places had nothing to show us in the way of
migration. No bird, indeed, need have wished to leave such a
tropical climate as we found there; the Chiff-chaff was in full
and vigorous song there on the 20th, and the Willow-wren
was also heard.

On the 21st we went on to Swanage in cooler weather,
with rain falling at intervals. Swanage is a good point for
watching the movements of such birds as pass along our

southern coast; for here ends abruptly that long line of down which includes Bindon Hill, and here too ends the long stretch of coast extending eastwards from Weymouth Bay. Birds which are pursuing either down or coast-line will, when they arrive at Swanage, have to consider what to do next: whether to turn up northwards to Poole harbour and Bournemouth, or to go straight across to the Isle of Wight, which on any clear day is distinctly visible. The result seems to be that the angle formed by Swanage Bay and the coast from St. Aldhelm's Head to Durlstone Point is sometimes as full as it can hold of birds in the autumn, and chiefly of Linnets, Pipits, and Wagtails, with a fair sprinkling of Warblers and Chats.

But the travelling of Swallows and Martins is what chiefly attracts me to this region. On 20th September 1887, while staying at Lulworth, half-way between Weymouth and Swanage, I discovered that every Swallow and Martin which I saw was steadily travelling eastwards. They travelled in parties of from fifty to two hundred, just as I had seen them in the Alps, and as they are described in the 'Migration Reports'. I could trace these parties for a long distance with my glass, as I stood on a long and narrow ridge of down some five hundred feet above the sea; their general direction was always due east, though they seemed to follow pretty closely the long line of the down, which curves somewhat inland eastwards from Lulworth. The whole day they continued to pass, not in a continuous stream, but in these great packs, which at one moment were over my head and all around me, and in two or three minutes had quietly slipped on full half a mile towards the east. They did not, of course, fly straight ahead in a direct route; they seemed to be ever dallying and circling round, or sweeping backwards; yet you only had to keep a vigilant eye on them to discover that they were all the time moving onwards, and travelling at a rate which I guessed to be not much less than ten miles an hour.

On that day the wind was easterly, and therefore dead against them; but it was a gentle breeze and they were able to fly without apparent effort at a considerable height. The next day the wind was stronger; and on the third day, if I recollect right, it was very keen and cold, and instead of soaring they changed their tactics and took to skimming low along the steep flanks of the down. From my post of vantage at the top I watched with interest the way in which these delicate little birds withstood and conquered the force of a strong head wind. I can see them even now creeping along the shaggy sunburnt sides of that noble breezy down, tacking this way and that, now deep in the grassy hollows, now steering swiftly upwards, now yielding to the gale for a moment in a backward curve, but ever steadily pressing onwards. Some preferred a belt of lower ground between the down and the sea; but I noticed that where this comes to an end and the down itself falls again in precipitous cliffs direct into the waves, they all turned inwards again, hugging the hill, and not venturing to cross even a mile or two of sea to the further arm of the bay in the face of such a wind.

All this was so interesting that I wondered that I had never observed the same thing during previous visits to Lulworth in September. Diaries kept during those visits were at hand, but showed no trace of any such migration. Possibly I had missed the exact days on which the birds were passing; but it is more likely, I think, that I simply failed to *notice* what was going on. The flight of these birds is so deviating that its general direction may very easily be missed, and in fact it is almost indispensable that the observer should be posted on some commanding height in order to appreciate it. I have seen the same kind of migration going on in the Midlands since that visit to Lulworth, but found it very difficult to follow and make sure of, owing to the want of such a point of vantage as that noble ridge of down.

On returning that autumn to my Oxfordshire home, I found that considerable parties of Swallows and Martins were passing over the village at intervals every forenoon. Our own birds, which regularly gather on my house roof for a week or two before they leave, had apparently departed; but from north and west fresh companies continued to arrive, and it was long before we felt that 'the Swallows had really gone'. These strangers lingered a while about the village, generally in the neighbourhood of the church, and then took their departure in a south-easterly direction along the line of our valley. But, as I have already said, it was difficult to trace their line of flight, and impossible to follow it for any distance, owing to the want of a commanding hill whence I could sweep the whole country with my glass. I may mention that one day at nightfall I found a small orchard in a neighbouring village crowded with them; and no doubt this was a detachment resting for the night, which would proceed on its way early next morning.

The following year, 1889, I discovered that Swanage is an even better place than Lulworth for 'taking the auspices' in the autumn. On the 6th of October, just before the Oxford term began, I was able to pay a hurried visit to Swanage to see an old pupil, whose family understand and indulge my proclivities with most hospitable kindness. When on the morning of the following day I reached the coast near Durlstone Point, I found the Swallow migration still going on, for a small party soon passed me and disappeared in an easterly direction. As they vanished the question occurred to me – What will they do when they reach the point where the coast turns northward at a sharp right angle? Will they follow it, or will they cross the sea to the Isle of Wight, or is this perhaps a point at which they boldly strike across to France? It began to dawn upon me, in fact, that this sudden turn in the line of the coast would surely raise a question in the minds of the birds as well as in mine, and I was extremely curious to see what they would do.

The question was soon answered. Walking nearer to Durlstone Point, I watched for another party, which was not long in coming. They passed by me, and, as they neared the headland, rose in the air higher and higher, not seeming to move onwards for a while, but simply circling round and rising, and then, at a great height, they set off over the sea in the direction of the Isle of Wight. I followed them with the glass till they were such tiny specks that it was painful to try and keep them in view. *The cliffs of the island were at this time very distinctly visible.* I watched one or two more parties follow in the same track; but I was not alone and could not stay long – my kind host was with me, and friendship forbade that I should weary him. It was not until the morning of the 9th that I was at liberty to spend an hour or two in the same spot *in solitude.*

As I left the house that morning the hills were hidden in a soft mist, nor could I see anything of the Isle of Wight; and it did not occur to me at the moment that this might have some effect on the course adopted by the birds. I was consequently rather taken by surprise, when I reached the cliffs about a mile west of Durlstone and watched the first party that passed me, to find that, instead of rising in the air and going out to sea, they turned back when they came near the headland, and still skimming close to the ground, and passing close to me as I sat sheltered from the wind under a wall, they made northwards over the hill towards the town of Swanage. After waiting a while, I saw another party take exactly the same course. They refused the sea-passage, and turned inland and northwards. The nature of the ground I was on prevented my watching them in this direction to any distance; and I could only stand there and wish that some kind wizard would turn me into a Swallow for but one hour, that I might follow in their track, and learn something of the ways and the minds of these little travellers. But it was a fair guess that, having refused the sea once, they would hug the land for some distance at least.

The sun had now come out, and I sat down to enjoy it while waiting for a third company of Swallows. All the birds I saw that morning, I may say, were Swallows, not Martins; and all of which I had a good view were young birds, so far as I could judge by their tails. Presently another series of ghostly little forms came gliding over me, and I at once jumped up and kept the binocular steadily on them as they went eastwards. But this company did not return inland as the others had done; like the party I had watched two days before, they rose in the air when they neared the point, and

circling higher and ever higher, as if observing and considering, they at length began to disappear over the sea.
I scrambled over a high loose stone wall, at the risk of
breaking my bones, in order to reach a higher point and keep
them longer in sight; and then it was that I discovered that
*the Isle of Wight had arisen out of the mist since I last was within view
of it.*

I scrambled over a high loose stone wall

Though I have been at Swanage several times since 1889,
I have never again caught the migration in full swing, or seen
a party of birds cross to the Isle of Wight; the weather has
been cold and rainy, and such parties as I have seen have
always kept to the coast. This was the case in the present
year, 1894, when the Swallows seemed all to be harking back
from Durlstone Point, though the island was generally
visible. The promontory was full of birds, and on all the
broken ground occupied by deserted Purbeck quarries the
Pipits and Linnets were in extraordinary numbers. The
Wagtails of course were here; and at Studland Bay, three
miles to the north, I was delighted to find all three species

together, the Pied, the Yellow, and the Grey, in a little flock which seemed to be working slowly along the shore.

On leaving Swanage we had yet one day of my nephews' holidays, and it chanced that we spent it at Bexhill, two or three miles west of Hastings. At this point many birds might have already crossed the Channel; but even here there was much travelling to the eastwards. Parties of Hirundines – nearly all of them Swallows, though I saw a single Sand-martin – were hurrying towards Hastings; the weather was heavy after a stormy night, and in a long stretch of wild ground to the west of the town the birds were threading the paths among the gorse and would suddenly appear round a corner within a a few feet of me, and fly almost between my legs. This reach of coast, which luckily has not been con-secrated as yet to the overweening devotees of golf, affords excellent shelter to migrating birds, and would probably be a good station for an observer both in spring and autumn. Wagtails, Linnets, Pipits, Stonechats and Wheatears were here that day (24th September); and a few Skylarks, who were probably going *westwards*.

Throughout our ten days travel we had seen nothing very startling in the movements of birds, nor any rare species. But a student of birds can find plenty to employ him in the haunts even of our most familiar companions. The one remarkable fact which met us at every place where we stayed – the fact which would probably have impressed itself most deeply on the mind of a foreign ornithologist – was the crowding and singing of Robins. Abundant as they are in autumn over the whole country, in the extreme south they seem to be closely packed in every garden, orchard, and hedgerow. And in spite of this abundance, which brought the song to my ears every hour and almost every minute I was out of doors, I found it impossible to weary of the strain; never has it seemed to me more rich and tender in tone, or more varied in execution and meaning.

I was unable to follow the birds farther, as I had intended, or to cross to the coast of France at the time they too might be crossing. Returning to the Midlands, I found Swallows,

Martins, and Pied Wagtails still here in large numbers; the Wagtails gathering in one field by the church, which they always frequent at this time, and the Swallows and Martins still crowding every sunny morning on my house roof. But it is quite plain that they are preparing to leave me; their flights seem to grow longer and longer, and if I did not follow them carefully with the glass I might fancy that they had utterly vanished. But however far they fly, and however high – and at this time they will sometimes soar to a very great height – I shall presently see them returning, and tomorrow morning the little black figures will be flitting before my bedroom window soon after the sun is up. The weather is calm, heavy, and not inclement, and the air is full of flies; and as long as there is neither hard frost, nor storm, nor a famine of insect food, we may expect to see these lingering reminiscences of the summer.

Yet I doubt whether we shall have them with us as late as in 1891, when I caught my last glimpse of a Swallow in Oxford on the morning of 23rd November. There will be more than four months this winter between the departure of the last Swallow and the appearance of the first Chiff-chaff. As I write this last paragraph (5th October) the wind has turned to the east, and brought cold rain with it. A large Gull, in immature plumage, has passed over the village in a north-easterly direction. Not a Warbler is to be seen anywhere; the Fieldfares and Redwings may be expected daily. We are getting ready for winter, and my summer studies are over.

In Praise of Rain

The essay 'In Praise of Rain' appeared in Part 1 of The Book of the Open Air, *edited by Edward Thomas, which was published in 1907.*

Thomas had studied history for two years at Lincoln College between 1900 and 1902 and must have become well acquainted with Fowler during that time; Fowler's friend, Horace Mann, recorded that Thomas told him that he knew no one who had a finer sense of the characteristics of the English countryside.

Certainly Fowler was extremely sensitive to the changes in the weather, and his writings contain countless references to the subject. Some of his finest descriptive writing concerns the heavy snowfalls of 1881 and 1908, which, together with accounts of a severe thunderstorm in 1910, and of the great drought of 1911, are included in Kingham Old and New.

In Praise of Rain

There is nothing more delightful than to look leisurely over a bridge

It is the privilege of the educated Englishman, unless he be a farmer or a market gardener, to think of rain as a nuisance. He does not understand his debt to it; he hardly knows what it is to long for it. It interferes with the out-of-door games that he loves, and it spoils his cycling or his motoring. But the fact is that the peculiar beauty of his country is more the result of rain than any other cause. It is rain, the gentle constant rain of the ocean, that has moulded his country into hill and dale, and made his roads twist and turn, mount and descend, ever giving him fresh scenes as he moves along them. It is this gentle rain, not coming in seasonal deluge, but spreading itself in fair proportion over the whole year, that has given such constant variety to his landscape, and has given himself the unconscious eye of an artist in contemplating it, and in suiting to it the works of his hands. The approach of rain, the passing of rain, the rain over and gone – all these phases have an educating power on his eye and mind, though he be unconscious of it. They are beautiful in themselves, and the changes they work in the atmosphere and on the earth keep his outdoor mind alive and stirring. They accustom his eye to see his landscape through a glorifying medium; they have given his painters a sense of atmospheric effects which perhaps belongs to no other nation, for in this moist land of ours the atmosphere is almost always visible between us and the object we look at in the distance.

And it is rain, spreading itself thus so constantly and so quietly over the moderate elevations of our land, that has made water an almost invariable accompaniment of our wayside scenes; our roads and lanes and footpaths are for ever crossing it, and bridges great and small are tempting the artist to set up his easel, or the wayfarer to lean on them and refresh his eyes with running water and its plants and animals. The motorist and cyclist shoot past these pleasant spots, but for the walker there is nothing more delightful than to look leisurely over a bridge. These streams seldom wholly dry up, like the torrents of Greece and the East; and in summer the wealth of their vegetation – a wealth that often almost hides them from view – is beyond my power to describe. Loosestrife, forget-me-nots, willow-herb, water-lilies, yellowflags, flowering rushes, are the embroidery that the kindly rain sets upon her daughters the streams.

We hardly know in this country what a drought is. The last I can remember was in 1893, lasting from the middle of March to the middle of May; I can well remember the intense relief when the moisture came at last. As a rule we have to learn the true value of rain from the Hebrew poetry, the only Eastern literature we read. The psalms are full of this lesson for a Western; and in the last poem written by the poet-king (2 Sam. xxiii. 5) it is expressed in a simile of exquisite beauty: the just king is 'as the tender grass springing out of the earth by clear shining after rain'.

There are of course different kinds of rain, of different degrees of pleasantness. There is the heavy downpour, sustained and perhaps depressing, in which it is not enjoyable to be out; yet this does excellent work in washing as well as in stimulating growth. After a spell of dry weather everything needs to be cleansed; and this rain carries away from the surface of the earth and the roads all that ought not to linger there, fills the streams and washes their beds and banks. Even if they flood there is seldom much harm done, and the refuse that is spread over the meadows when the flood retires sinks into the ground and helps to enrich it. Then there is the soft warm rain that makes all nature rejoice, plants and animals alike – *neish* rain, as we call it, or used to call it, in the west; even man can be out and enjoy himself in this rain, for it makes all other things happy and fragrant, and can do himself no harm. But the most beautiful of all rain is that which comes in showers – showers of which nature drinks quietly and earnestly for a while, and then seems to lift a smiling face in grateful content as the sun comes out on her. In the spring of 1906 we had but few of those exquisite days of warm sun and soft shower from the west, which are so peculiarly English that to be without them in April and May is like being deprived of our birthright. And lastly, in contrast with these delicious showers there is yet another rain, distilling itself from cloud and mist on our western hills for many days together, hindering rather than helping the works of man, if not of other living things, and reminding us that neither rain without sun or sun without rain can do for us and nature exactly what we wish. In a Cumberland dale I have seen the whole population making hay, while the sun was shining on a Sunday morning, with the full sanction of their good parson, who postponed his service for their benefit, and finally preached a sermon of extraordinary eloquence and power to a congregation of two strangers and his sexton. Those strangers soon found that they must accept the drizzle and make the best of it, and that all attempts to counteract it by umbrellas and mackintoshes are vain and even harmful – for they do but keep reminding you that it is raining.

It is true then that the sweet and even distribution of rain over the greater part of this island has it exceptions; there is no part of England that has as a rule too little rain, but there are districts which get too much, and where man loses the constant sense of wholesome change, and the frequent cheering influence of the sun.

But let us return to the lower lands, where rain rarely continues for many days together, and watch the subtle influence it has on the life of plants and animals. All plants must have water, and many of them will droop after a day or two of dry heat; then, when the rain comes, it is almost possible to see the grass growing. The processes that go on at the roots and in the stems and leaves are hidden from us; but it is interesting to note the different ways in which different kinds of plants deal with the rain as it falls on their leaves. Some adorn themselves with it, retaining it in the form of gems sparkling in the sunshine, and thus make themselves more beautiful than ever to the human eye; others distribute it over their leaves as moisture hardly discernible unless we look at them closely; and some few seem almost to reject it. As you walk along a road during or just after a shower, looking into the hedgerows (always a most soothing occupation for eye and mind), and chance to be thinking of this treatment of rain by the plants, you can hardly fail to be struck by the surly and inhospitable conduct of the whole nettle tribe – a tribe that flourishes in dry places – and seems to be none the worse for dust and drought. The nettle leaves seem really to reject the rain; you may look in vain for a leaf which clearly shows the moisture upon it, and if you closely watch the drops falling, they seem to vanish and come to nothing as they reach these dark forbidding structures. Yet underneath them the long swordgrass is sparkling with a thousand diamonds; so is the clover, and the beautiful silverleaf, and above them the wild rose and the honeysuckle both keep these brilliant gems for a short while. It might almost seem as if the plants that we love best have this way of decking themselves out, while those that we value least have never acquired it; for I notice that neither the docks nor the tall acrid buttercup can use the rain to please the human eye. But this is fancy, and for the real facts and the reasons for them, which are doubtless to be found in the varying structure of the leaves and the nature of their surfaces, we must go to the professed botanist. I have lately noticed that of all the plants in my garden the lupins, even with their small pointed leaves, which look as though they never could retain a drop, had decorated themselves more beautifully than all their neighbours. I put a lupin leaf under a strong magnifying glass, and found the surface softly hairy; but this does not carry me very far. Experiments with a watering-pot as well as the magnifying glass might tell us something more.

No one needs to be told how wholesome for the life of birds is a shower of rain; they let us know it themselves by breaking out into song the moment the rain has passed. I seem to notice that this is more particularly the case with our resident species, less so perhaps with those that have come from hot climates to bring up their young in cooler regions. Few of these summer migrants will sing actually during the rain, while the blackbird, song-thrush, missel-thrush, robin, may always be heard if the rain is not too hard and cold. Yesterday (16th May) we had the first soft rain – fragrant rain, as I like to call it – that we have enjoyed for weeks, and while it was falling the blackbirds were wonderfully voiceful, and, as I fancied, unusually mellow. The sweet monotonous song of the missel-thrush is often to be heard while a wet gale is blowing; but the whitethroats and whinchats and black-caps, which have only lately joined us, seem to like to wait till the rain is over. I am not so often out in rain for long together that I can speak with entire confidence on this point; but if it be so, the reason probably is that the insect-eaters like the sun best, the grub-eaters the rain.

But it is not only the song and the food of our native birds that is affected by the rain supply; some of them need it for their masonry as well. In a very dry spring neither thrush nor blackbird can line his nest with mud, and I have heard of cases in which they had for once in a way to do without it. Swallows too, and housemartins, must have mud for the structure of their nests, and their nesting operations may be delayed for weeks by dry east wind and hot sun; in such a year we may look out for young martins still in the nests well into October. If the spell of drought is broken by a thunder shower it is pleasant to see the swallow tribe instantly busy on the roads or by the pond side – but a single shower too often only raises false hopes of progress.

The grass was adorned by many varieties of the common little snail

In the rain of yesterday the grass in the hedgerows was adorned not only by the watery gems, but also by the many varieties of the common little snail which we all know so well on the downs, and in all short sweet pastures they were climbing up all long stalks even to the very top, as if from a desire to get right into the full favour of the rain. Indeed all creeping things, except perhaps the viper, enjoy the moisture, which rids them of dust and all the grittiness that comes of drought. Lately in period of east winds and frost it was pitiable to see worms covered with grit and gravel wriggling on the path, plagued no doubt with parasites, loathsome even to the birds, which never seem to touch them in this state; now if I see a worm on the road, – and after rain they are out all night on the roads, and even longer – they are clean and wholesome, without a particle of gravel sticking to them. In the garden the frogs and toads, as well as snails, come out and revel in the dampness, and the tortoise, if you have one, knows that he will find his food succulent. The most wonderful exhibition of reptile life that I have ever seen was not in England, but on a Swiss Alp, which became alive after rain with fat, jolly little salamanders, all crowding and tumbling upon each other, and with their jet-black skins shining with moisture.

One kind of living creature does not relish rain – I mean the fully developed insects. But in the early stages of their career they have owed so much to rain and moisture, that in later life they have to take things as they come. The larvae of all insects are themselves moist, and need moisture to give them bodily comfort and the vegetable matter on **which** they feed. Caterpillars must have their food-plant, **which** cannot grow without moisture; so that when we see the Mayflies crushed by a thunder shower, or miss the butterflies on a wet day, we have to reflect that they would be neither Mayflies nor butterflies if it had not been for the kindly rain. As to spiders, I am half inclined to guess that they are abnormal and dislike rain from infancy upwards; but this I must leave to the specialist.

So it would seem that man, and almost all if not quite all the creatures that live around him, are the better for rain and ought to enjoy it. Long ago we used to be afraid of it, and even for an ordinary walk young ladies used to take some time to 'get ready'. The little heroine of that delightful novel *Northanger Abbey* could not walk by the Avon at Bath with Henry Tilney and his sister because it came on to rain; and it is pathetic to contemplate her grief as she watched the first drops on the window panes. 'Oh dear, I do believe it will be wet,' broke from her in a most despairing tone. In these days healthy English men, women, boys and girls, do not mind rain. Last spring, landing on the coast of Asia Minor, a hundred and fifty of us, old and young, were wetted through by a thunderstorm in ten minutes; we pushed on, and no one seemed to mind. Here, in the sweet gentle rain of the Atlantic, we ought to be quite content. And we need be in no hurry to get home quickly, if we would see the earth and all its creatures rejoicing under the genial influence of the moisture.

Kingham Old and New

Of Fowler's last book on natural history and the country-side, published in 1913, his sixty-fifth year, E. V. Lucas wrote in the Spectator: *'This book is human to the core. And more than merely human, it has personality and an underlying tenderness and sense of the best in life that makes it literature. Between the lines on every page one catches glimpses of one who loves his fellow men, and has acquired rich stores of sunny wisdom and sympathy from an observant life of tranquil delight in nature, books and neighbours.' Lucas went on to rank* Kingham Old and New *alongside Thoreau's* Walden *and* Cranford *as an example of the best in rural literature. Other journals chose to draw a parallel with* Selborne, *among these being a reviewer in the* Athenaeum: *'In the beautiful limpidity of his style and the mingling in him of the antiquary and the naturalist he often makes us think of Gilbert White.'*

Birds, Past and Present

They used to take nuts out of a tumbler

As I read once more – not without the pleasure of a parent in contemplating his first-born – my ancient book, *A Year with the Birds*, I find that much of what is there said about the birds of Kingham and Oxford does not strictly hold good of the Kingham or Oxford of the twentieth century. This is not owing to any fault of mine; it is the fault of the birds themselves, or rather, perhaps of some facts in their life-history which are entirely hidden from us at present. True, the majority of *residents*, with one exception to be mentioned directly, are much as they were when I wrote my book in 1885–6; but two or three of the most familiar and welcome migrants have almost disappeared from our fields and streams. The fact, disappointing as it is, is none the less an interesting one; for the gradual increase or decrease of the numbers of a species in a particular locality depends on circumstances most difficult to determine. Here is one of the many fascinating problems of ornithology, and one to which too little attention has been paid by observers. For example, for many years past neither Grey Wagtails nor Green Sandpipers have been regular autumn visitors. A Wagtail may appear now and again, but makes no stay; and the Sandpipers have almost entirely deserted us. I have only seen one of recent years, and that was in the pure little stream on the further side of Churchill Heath wood.

Although, as I noted, the birds in former days did not seem to be disgusted by the occasional pollution of the water, it is possible that one horrible inundation of poison in 1898 created some permanent prejudice in their minds. This occurred on Good Friday of that year. Some one asked me early in the morning to go and look at the brook. I found it in a condition which caused me instantly to write to the Chipping Norton authorities, and the same thing has never happened again. The black mud-banks were covered with the heads of wretched gudgeon innumerable, protruded out of the water because it was too poisonous for them to breathe. I imagine that every fish in the brook was killed that morning; for in the afternoon I found the water, the whole way to the point where it joins the Evenlode, covered with the floating corpses of these miserable victims. Near this point, and just by a weir over which the water falls some eight or ten feet, I had been watching a pair of Grey Wagtails who were obviously thinking of nesting there, and was congratulating myself on the probability of a record almost unique in our county. But the stench of the water was too much for them, and they went elsewhere, probably to some clear wholesome Cotswold stream. It is, however, a curious fact that though the water has for many years been perfectly pure, the Sandpipers have never come back again, and the Grey Wagtails have never attempted to nest, and have very rarely visited the brook.

I pass to a most remarkable example of change in the

numbers of a species, for it includes *both an increase and a decrease* within my own memory. When I first began to notice birds here and at Oxford in the seventies, the Yellow Wagtail was not by any means abundant, so far as I can recollect; and I do not think I can be wrong, for in those days, when I was learning to recognise the birds with immense ardour in solitary walks, I can hardly have overlooked such conspicuous and charming creatures as these. But in a few years they began to press themselves on my attention all the summer through, and in the spring of 1887 (28th April) I saw a wonderful assembly of them on Port Meadow at Oxford.

For the next few years I regularly looked out for them on the great meadow, and never failed to find plenty, with one or two of their continental blue-headed cousins among them. All these years they were abundant at Kingham, and, indeed, in all suitable places wherever I happened to be.

During these years of their abundance these little birds made every summer walk delightful. They were running about among the feet of the cattle, or perching on telegraph wires, on high branches of trees, or even on the ears of wheat, which hardly bent beneath their weight. Their cheerful little silvery note was so familiar all round us, that I have known a Sedge-warbler mock it with persistence and success, and the Marsh-warbler would occasionally indulge in the same pastime.

But in 1894 I had already noted a diminution in their numbers, and ever since then there has been no question about it. I still look out for them on Port Meadow, and, indeed, on both sides of the river, but even in April they are few and far between. This year, 1912, I have only seen one. I do not see them in the Parks, or in a spot near Marston copse where they were once always to be found. At Kingham I see more during their autumn migration than at any time in spring or summer; then they flock with the Pied Wagtails and roost in the big osier-bed. But in June the joyous little yellow sprites no longer dance about the hay, or pick up the flies stirred by the feeding cattle.

I can give no explanation of this singular change. Man can have had no share in bringing it about: the nests are very hard to find, and our boys, even if they found them, would not take the eggs. Everything in Oxfordshire is as it was twenty years ago, so far as these birds are concerned, in the condition of our rural economy, and they can have nothing to complain of. We must be content to confess our ignorance of the causes which increase or diminish their numbers; but some day, when our scientific ornithologists are less absorbed in the discovery of new species in far away lands, and of varying forms of species at home and in Europe, they will find time to attack a problem, the very difficulty of which lends it attraction.

Another case needing investigation is that of the Landrail or Corncrake, which used to be extremely common, while now its 'crake' is seldom heard. My dog put one up in a field where the barley was still standing, 4th October, 1912, and having the bird in my mind, I asked a boy on my way home (the same boy who found the Stonechats' nests) whether he knew the 'crake', imitating it for him. He did not recognise it in the least. The numbers of this species are liable to much change, probably owing to the fluctuation of the date of hay-harvest; an early harvest will destroy the nests. In some counties the numbers have been recently well maintained.

Before I go on to another clear example of this curious upward and downward curve in the numbers of a species visiting and breeding in this county, let me remark that whatever be the cause, the Wild Birds' Protection Act, and its application by a County Council, can have nothing to do with it. In Oxfordshire we have never asked for power to protect these small migrants, believing, rightly as I think, that they do not need it, and that such protection would only be creating small crime with no profit to man or bird. The great increase in the numbers of the Yellow Wagtail between about 1885 and 1895 came about after the first Act had been passed, but without help from it in this county. These Acts are of some use in checking attacks on rare and obvious birds, such as Hawks and Owls, and possibly of some very limited value in preserving Bullfinches and Goldfinches. But the vast majority of our small birds, especially the summer migrants, attract little notice and call for no protection, and I would earnestly advise those warm-hearted but ill-informed persons, who from time to time write to the Society for the Protection of Birds, drawing terrible but imaginary pictures of depredations committed, to study the facts patiently and coolly. The explanation of those facts does not lie in Oxfordshire and England, or in anything man does there, but in the Great Sahara and the African regions to the south of it, and in the weather in the Mediterranean at the time of migration. But even about this last possibility there is a difficulty: bad weather in migration time should effect many species, not one or two only: for many are travelling just about the same time.

Sometimes, let us remember, a species will increase or decrease as the result of its own vitality or want of vitality, and of its power or want of power to adapt itself to new conditions of life. I can give examples of both increase and diminution brought about in this way.

A few years ago the Redshank was hardly known in this county or in Berkshire. When Mr. Aplin published his *Birds of Oxfordshire*, a book of remarkable and accurate knowledge, he wrote of the Redshank as only an occasional visitor, seen now and again in the winter, adding that there is a single specimen in the Oxford Museum, labelled as shot on Port Meadow. But in June 1905 I heard of Redshanks breeding near Bablock Hithe, and made a solitary expedition one morning to make sure of them: and on the 13th of that month Mr. Aplin himself, wishing to see the sight with his own eyes, accompanied me there and satisfied himself. Since then this beautiful bird has become well known to all ardent ornithologists in Oxford, as breeding regularly in several places along the river above Oxford and elsewhere. On 2nd April, 1910, I was even able to record it as occurring at Kingham, but it was then only resting for the night on its way to its breeding-grounds. There can be no doubt that this is a vigorous species, and it seems also to be an adventurous one, pushing into new districts and settling comfortably in new quarters.

Now let us take, by way of contrast, a little bird that is comparatively weak and delicate, the Dartford Warbler; one which seems only to be able to exist on furzy heaths in thick cover, and whose wings are so short and small that it can do little more than creep about in this cover, flitting rather than flying when it does take wing. I happen to know it well, for I once had the good luck on two successive days to watch it feeding its young on the great heath between Wareham and Poole harbour in Dorset. In the very hard winters of 1880–1, and 1886–7, it must have suffered severely, for it was rarely seen after those years: but it is now again holding its own in the southern counties in suitable places. There is evidence that some years ago a few pairs existed in the gorse on Shotover and near Stow Wood, but I myself have never seen it in this county, in spite of careful search. Protection for such a bird as this might be of some use: but it would be protection against those who should be its friends, not against the much defamed schoolboy, who would neither notice the bird nor find its nest. If its numbers decrease, if it dies out altogether in counties like ours, which are ill suited to its needs, the cause will be a natural one, arising from its own weakness, and it is most improbable, that any amount of legislation will be of use in such a case. The most likely place for it near Oxford is the great hollow to the south-west of Shotover, now happily the property of the University; and I think we may be confident that any one finding it there will look on it as university property, and respect it accordingly.

But let us return from this digression to take another example of the double curve of which I was speaking just now. In 1885, I wrote of the Redstart as having become abundant in recent years. In commenting on this fact I came to the same conclusion which I stated just now, that the increase of Redstarts must be put down to causes taking effect beyond the sea.

This remarkable increase was fully maintained for some years. Oxford and its precincts, especially Mesopotamia and all river-banks with pollard willows, became full of them. My garden at Kingham always had a pair nesting in a hole in an old apple-tree, until they were evicted by Starlings, which in their turn gave way to Blue Tits. And however far afield I went, I never failed to find Redstarts. Yet recently the numbers have been steadily decreasing; the familiar gentle song, with its peculiar and unmistakable *timbre*, is seldom heard in Mesopotamia: my garden has long ago been deserted: in my walks about the village and the neighbouring parishes it is now quite an event for me to see a Redstart. The other day I met a friend who lives at Charlbury, half-way between Kingham and Oxford: he stopped and asked me if I had seen a Redstart this year, for he himself had seen not one.

At one time I was inclined to think that this decrease might be due to a want of suitable nesting-holes, caused by an increase in numbers of the Starling and consequent difficulties in house-hunting; and I still think that this may possibly be a contributing cause, though not the main one. This notion seemed to be borne out by a note in the Migration Committee's Report of 1906, drawing attention to the curiously uneven distribution of the Redstart, which was fairly common in Wales, and the north of England (where the Starling is, or was, far less abundant than with us), while it was exceptionally scarce in the south and east. Perhaps the Starling and Sparrow between them, two species which are over-abundant and aggressive in the southern corn-lands of our island, may have something to answer for in the case of the Redstart: but without more substantial evidence I do not like to jump to this conclusion. After consulting a number of county books of ornithology I am inclined to think that when, from some reason which we cannot get at, the Redstart population is larger than usual, when, that is, the numbers reaching us from abroad are great, the whole of England has to find them quarters: but when, as in recent years, the numbers are below the average, they go on to those breeding-grounds which really suit them best – the woods and hills of Wales and the north.

The Nuthatch is another most interesting instance of diminution in numbers, though not, so far as I can remember, of increase before diminution. About the diminution there is, I am certain, no doubt whatever, in this county, but I cannot answer for it in other parts. At Kingham we used to have many pairs in the village, and my old friend Colonel Barrow's last years were much enlivened by the constant attendance of Nuthatches at his window, where they used to take nuts out of a tumbler, and carry them off to some undisclosed treasure-house. I have some reason to think that there is still a pair in the village, but I have no personal evidence of it. I never now hear that bright loud self-confident whistle of theirs in spring, or the sweet bubbling note which announced the season of pairing.

These same pleasant and cheerful sounds used to be heard in Christ Church Meadow and other places within the Oxford precincts, but so far as my own experience goes they are now far less familiar. Any other witnesses besides myself combine with my own evidence to force me to the conclusion that, in spite of its hardihood, this bird is far more of a rarity than it used to be. My neighbour, Lord Moreton, for example, tells me that they have a single pair at Sarsden, where they once had some twenty. Mr. Aplin is of much the same opinion as regards the Bloxham district. On the other hand writers in the *Zoologist*, in response to a question of mine, have denied that in their districts, e.g. in Kent, the bird is less common than of old.

In our own county the problem of explaining the diminution ought to be a simple one, for the bird is not a migrant and the cause must be near at hand, if we could but hit on it. But there has been no change that would seriously affect the Nuthatches. There is still plenty of suitable timber, plenty of old apple trees with holes in which they might nest, and I cannot say that I have personal evidence of their eviction from these by Starlings, though it is possible that some years back, when Starlings were increasing by leaps and bounds, this may have happened without my observing it. I do not think that either men or boys, either collectors or mere depredators, can be held responsible. I do, indeed, remember one case in which it was believed that mischievous boys had plastered up a Nuthatch's hole in my village, out of pure 'cussedness': but as the accusers were unaware of the fact that the Nuthatch invariably plasters up its hole for itself, always leaving a very small aperture for ingress and egress, I believe that the much maligned schoolboy was here, as so often, innocent.

What then can the cause be? A total failure of the nut-crop for a year or two might make some difference to the race; but then we must remember that for about half the year the Nuthatch does not feed on nuts, but on the insects, pupae, etc., which are to be found in the bark of trees, and it could probably subsist on these even if it were deprived of nuts in the autumn and winter. I fear that even in this case the cause of diminution is hidden from us. We can make one or two guesses: we can remember the recent epidemic among Woodpigeons, and guess that something of the same kind has befallen our Oxfordshire Nuthatches. Some years ago there was an almost complete disappearance of squirrels from our woods which was probably caused by disease; they have now picked up again, and we may hope the same for the Nuthatches. In 1887 the crayfish of our Thames tributaries were smitten with an epidemic, from which, so far as I know, their numbers have never really recovered. Previous to this epidemic they were so abundant in the Thames and its tributaries that a regular industry of making crayfish-pots flourished in many places. But as regards the Nuthatches, unless some one more observant or ingenious than myself will suggest a convincing answer to the puzzle I must give it up.

Now I turn to a bird which, of recent years, has entirely deserted the city of Oxford, and which I also fail now to find at Kingham, the Reed-warbler. I have, indeed, no reason to suppose that its numbers have seriously diminished. It is still plentiful, I believe, along the banks of the Isis, and in the reed-beds near Wolvercote; and its absence from our Kingham osier-beds is not by any means conclusive, for I have only known it there as a straggler, and I do not think the Evenlode suits it as do Isis and Cherwell, which are more sluggish streams with greater abundance of reeds. But as regards Oxford the facts are interesting, and admit of easy explanation.

When I first began to notice Oxford birds, the Cherwell was an almost unknown river. I well remember my first voyage of exploration beyond Parsons' Pleasure. Just above the bathing-place we were hailed by a man in a punt, who demanded sixpence for admission to the higher reaches; this my companion, a barrister from London of powerful build and obstinate character, sternly refused to pay, and we went on. But on our return we found the enemy's punt moored across the stream, and himself armed with a long boat-hook to arrest our progress. Then ensued a terrific naval battle, watched with immense delight by bathers drying themselves on the bank, who naturally took our side and cheered loudly every charge we made. The water was ploughed up in the struggle, and tempers waxed hot, but at last, after several failures, we dodged the boat-hook and slipped away down stream in triumph. The scene is photographed on my memory: but I only mention it here to show how little the Cherwell was navigated, and what peaceful retreats it offered to the birds.

A little way above the bathing-place, in the jungle at the bottom of the Parks, I first made acquaintance with the Reed-warbler's crooning soliloquy. There, year after year, I watched for it in May, and knew that it was breeding though I would not disturb its nest. Then, when I was thoroughly familiar with it, I began to find it in other places, some of them surprising ones; not only in suitable spots by our rivers, but some distance away from them. For example, for several years the song was to be heard from lilac bushes in the plantation now mainly occupied by the physiological laboratories. Another favourite place was a bush just outside the Botanic Gardens, and opposite the schools of St. Peter's in the East. In the little copse at the Cherwell end of the Broad Walk a nest was built for several years in succession in a tall privet bush, secure from all invasion. It seemed as if the Reed-warblers were beginning to form new habits: the charms of Oxford were so great that they were willing to forgo their favourite reeds if they could find some shelter in our hallowed precincts.

On our return we found the enemy's punt moored across the stream

But then the Cherwell began to come into fashion, and to lose the last syllable of its name – for familiarity breeds contempt even in the use of language, and I doubt whether many undergraduates are now aware that it ever possessed a second syllable. Dons began to keep boats on its banks: ladies' colleges claimed it as their own, and all the summer term it became a scene of enjoyment for pleasure-loving youth and pensive middle age. The Reed-warblers quietly withdrew from these gay haunts, and also from the brick and mortar at the Museum. I should be glad to know whether they are still to be found farther up the Cherwell, or whether we must go to the upper river for them, and more especially to the somewhat lonely stretches between Bablock Hithe and Eynsham. The last place in which I have heard them close to the city is a dismal spot just beyond those water-logged cottages opposite the towing-path between Hithe Bridge and the North-Western Railway. As I said just now, it does not follow that because they have deserted the city their numbers have diminished in these parts; nor do I in the least blame any one for driving them away: doubtless they can find plenty of comfortable housing in less frequented spots. But looking back over some five and thirty years, it is interesting to note how a change in the fashions and habits of human beings can affect those of the birds. And I hope I may be excused for pointing out, as a phenomenon worth notice, that all this has happened in a period in which what is now called 'nature study' has come into vogue – in' which scores of popular books on natural history, and more especially about birds, have been published: societies founded for the protection of birds and plants, and Acts of Parliament for the same purposes passed and loudly proclaimed. I hold my tongue: I never complain of the inevitable: when I see a happy youth or maiden (or both) moored in a punt under the identical bush where once the Reedwarbler loved and sung, I can but murmur that where their ignorance is bliss, 'tis folly in me to be wise.

I will conclude this retrospect with a brief account of the most singular case of increase and subsequent diminution of a species which I have ever met with: but it differs from the examples already mentioned in being limited not only to a single parish, but almost to a single spot. It has the advantage of being easy to explain; and it will serve to illustrate the conditions under which an uncommon and delicate species may fix itself in a particular breeding-place, flourish there and increase in numbers for some years, yet eventually find itself in adverse circumstances, and die out or at least abandon the position.

In June 1889 I first made acquaintance in Switzerland with the Marsh-warbler. I listened to its delightful song at Meiringen on the banks of the Aar, but failed to find a nest, not knowing then exactly where to look for it. Two years later, in company with Mr. Aplin, I found the nest and eggs, which no one can mistake who has once seen them: this was near Interlaken, between the town and the lake of Brienz: a few days later we found another nest near Stanzstadt, which, like the first one, was hung in the stems of the meadow-sweet. By the time we left Switzerland, we were thus pretty well familiar with the song, appearance, habits, and nesting, of this species, which up to that time had so seldom been found in England that even good ornithologists were apt to doubt its existence as a British species.

Next year, I heard the song of the Marsh-warbler in the corner of an osier-bed within ten minutes' walk of my house at Kingham. This bed of osiers had been planted within my own recollection – indeed I can remember skating on frozen flood on the site of it: this bird was therefore in all likelihood not an old visitor which I had previously missed, but a stray individual in search of comfortable quarters for nesting. I summoned Mr. Aplin, and he at once recognised the unmistakable and delightful song. We spent a hot morning there searching for a nest, but neither then nor later in the month did we succeed in finding it. Possibly the male bird failed to find a mate: and indeed, it has always been a mystery to me that when individuals are so scarce it should be possible for a cock to attract a hen to a particular spot: one would fancy that the chances are a hundred to one against him. Of two facts later observation made me certain: that the cock arrives without a mate, and that he sings with extraordinary vigour and persistence for many hours a day on his arrival.

The next year, 1893, the osiers had been cut, and offered no great attraction in the way of cover, and after much listening I gave up all hope of seeing my little visitor again. Great was my delight when on the 20th of June I found that he had taken possession of another osier-bed about half a mile away, which was overgrown and neglected, comparatively dry, and with small open spaces here and there, such as this bird always likes to have about him. It was (and is) a small plot, not too big for a search, and just under a railway embankment which enabled me to sit and watch from a convenient height above it. Here I soon found a nest, which is now in the Oxford Museum. I was sharply criticised for taking it, but I was confident that the birds would build again, and it turned out that I was right. They returned to this spot next year, but I was away from home most of June, and made no progress in observing them.

In 1895 the birds were here again in June, evidently enjoying the cover which the still neglected osiers gave them; and I again found a nest on the 23rd. In 1896 I found yet another, and watched the progress of the nestlings until 22nd July, learning in the course of a month more about the species than any one in England then knew, except, perhaps the late Mr. H. Seebohm. In 1897 there seemed to be two birds singing, but I was away from home and could not trust the work of watching to any one else. In 1898 I found no less than three nests, all with eggs; one of these is that remarkable one with a cuckoo's egg fixed under the lining, which I took and presented to the Museum, as the first Marsh-warbler's nest in which a cuckoo in this country had played her accustomed trick.

Clearly the conditions were suiting the birds, which were otherwise lucky in avoiding the dangers of migration and returning to the place of their birth: for so, I think, we can best explain the increased number of families. In 1899 I was not able to do much in the way of searching, and only know that there was, at least, one nest in the osiers. The next year showed that the numbers had not diminished. That year, 1900, I knew of three nests and suspected a fourth, but the osier-bed had now been so long neglected that I was unable to search effectively in the tangle of undergrowth. In the autumn of that year the place was sold, and the new owner intended to cultivate the osiers properly, which meant cutting them in the spring.

This I knew would probably drive the birds away, and I interceded with him for them, with the result that he promised to leave them a bit of cover for next year's nesting. But from this time forward the fortunes of the little colony began to decline. I never found more than one nest in a year after this: it seemed as if the bit of cover left them at one end of the osiers could suffice for no more.

Yet in 1903 I found that beside the one pair that continued to find accommodation in the osier-bed one other pair, at least, was trying to nest elsewhere. They tried cow-parsnip, nettles, and other tall plants growing under the railway bank close by: but here they were exposed to misfortunes that had never befallen them in their old haunts. In the osiers no one ever discovered them but myself or my chosen friends: I have known a ploughboy take his rest and his midday meal within three yards of a nest, and never think of looking for one. But the plants in which they were now driven to hang their beautiful nests were cut down with the rest of the grass on the railway banks, and made into hay. Then, alas, my friend the farmer who owned the osiers forgot his promise and cut them all down in the spring of 1904, and this was the crown of their disasters. After trying to effect their nesting in a field of beans (where I found distinct traces of an attempt to string the bean-stems together as they had been used to do with meadowsweet or osiers), and also as I felt sure, in a wheat-field, they seemed to give it up as a bad job, and in 1905 I heard no more singing in or around that osier-bed. Next year there was a single pair in the other, where I had originally discovered them thirteen years before: but here they were disturbed by men working at a new bit of line hard by, and since then they have entirely disappeared from our neighbourhood. I have searched at the right time in the old places and in many others for miles around, but all in vain. But since then an observer not so very far away, in Worcestershire, has recorded the formation of a little colony, and it is particularly interesting to me to find that his birds did actually succeed in hanging their nest among the stalks of corn and charlock in a field of wheat, and that another pair had tried, unsuccessfully, like mine, to make bean-stalks serve their purpose.

And now for the moral of this tale, and indeed, of much that I have said in this chapter. Birds have inherited traditional habits of nesting, and if you can secure that they shall find conditions suitable to these habits, they will probably increase in numbers in a particular spot or district. If, on the other hand, you fail to provide them with what they want, they will be discouraged, decrease in numbers, and finally desert you. If I had been able to purchase that now historical little osier-bed, and so to keep it in a condition suited to their needs, I make no doubt that I should still be enjoying their singing every June, and enjoying too, the pride and privilege of admitting trusted friends to the sacred precincts. I may close this retrospect with the remark, most satisfactory to me and most creditable to human nature, that though I took many friends and Oxford pupils to those precincts, not a single one ever betrayed my secret, or brought a visitor without letting me know beforehand: and whatever damage was done to the interests of my Marsh-warblers was done by human beings unwittingly, and in pursuance of their own duties. Neither farmer, nor plough-boy, nor plate-layer on the line ever for a moment entertained the smallest ill-will towards them.

Postscript, September 1912

The foregoing chapter was written before any of our spring migrants had thought of returning to our shores. So far as I have been able to observe this spring, I find the following facts worth noting:

1. The species that is steadily on the increase, as indeed it has been for several years, is the Willow-wren, with whose gentle meditative strain all our woods were musical in May.

2. The Swallows were abundant, but the House-martins were late in arriving and, on the whole, few in numbers.

3. The Tree-pipit, which for several years I rarely saw here, has increased in numbers this summer, and several pairs have nested along the railway.

4. No Redstarts appeared in the spring, but just lately I have occasionally seen a young bird showing his red tail in a hedge.

5. The Red-backed Shrike, which used to be fairly well distributed, but was rare last year, has only been seen by me once this season.

6. Yellow Wagtails have been very scarce, except after the moult, when I used to see three or four in the flooded meadows.

To make up for these shortcomings we have had a pleasant surprise. A pair of Stonechats, for the first time in our records, brought off a brood in April by the road-side near Churchill Heath farm; I saw old and young together. They tried for a second brood in June, and were robbed of their young, probably by a stoat or weasel, for the nest was not disturbed though the eggs were gone. This nest was in a well-concealed hole in a bank facing away from the road, and would certainly not have been found if my young friend William Nash, had not just then been in charge of cows along the road-side pasture. The same boy ten days later detected another nest which this persevering couple had built, this time (strange to say) only a couple of feet from the road, in grass at the roots of a very tiny thorn-bush. Six eggs were laid again, and all was going well, when a road-mender (not of Kingham parish, I am glad to say) came this way, and in an idle moment chopped down the little bush and unwittingly destroyed the nest and eggs. Yet after all these little heroes made yet another nest! I was myself away in Edinburgh but the same intelligent boy assured me that this time they met with no disasters; and I do not doubt him, for by this time he had come to know them well, and was all along deeply interested in their fortunes.

Some Flowering Plants of Kingham

My doctor, an old and valued friend, nearly ran me over

Kingham lies in what may be called a basin – the wide basin of the Upper Evenlode, whose two tributaries have here formed considerable valleys to east and west of the main stream, giving the whole region, as seen from the hills around us, the appearance of a plain rather than a valley. To this feature of the country is mainly due its healthy breezy climate, which is cold without being too cold. It is a delightful country for an active man to live in, whether he hunts or cycles or humbly walks, as I do; and my long walks with Colonel Barrow, usually to some point on the hills, to east or west of us, were chiefly what fascinated me forty years ago, and fixed me here in time as a resident. True, if our walks had been limited to roads, I might have cared less about the life here; but I soon found that one great glory of Kingham is in the footpaths that lead in every direction, which are not merely short cuts from one point to another, but often stretch away over grass-fields for miles, without once bringing you to the sight of a road. Take, for example, the footpath to Bledington; it crosses the Evenlode and two railways, takes you up to the village, and leads to the extremely interesting church of Bledington by a short fragment of road: then plunges into a vast region of pasture, across which for two miles or so you must trace it with some discrimination, till you begin to climb the Cotswold ridge, and find yourself at last on a road again at the village of Westcote. I have known our late rector, who as a hunting man knew every field here as well as he knew his own garden, completely lost in a fog in this solitary region, when returning on foot from a call. He was forced to find his way back again up the hill to a road.

The villages of Icomb and Fifield can be reached in much the same way, and the latter ramble has greater variety, as the path passes through a part of Bruern Wood before it mounts the Cotswold slope towards Fifield and the Merry-mouth Inn. To east and north of us the roads are more handy and the paths less far-reaching: and the road up to White Quar is comparatively free from motors, for which a walker hard of hearing has now to be constantly on the look-out. Just here, however, as I was mounting this very hill, my doctor, an old and valued friend, nearly ran over me some time ago; and promised that if he did not end me in this way, he would at least mend me for nothing. But there is no need to stick to the road, here or anywhere, unless the fields be very miry in a wet season; for whether or not there are footpaths, no discreet walker, who understands the farmer's needs and wishes, should ever meet with any opposition to his free passage over the fields. To me all farmers and all land-owners have been uniformly benevolent for the last forty years and more. If I meet a farmer unknown to me when I am so trespassing, I almost always have a question to ask him which leads to a pleasant talk. The last one I met was in Icomb parish, where I happened to be prowling about after nests and plants; he told me two interesting facts – first, that a certain plant grew in the field where we were standing, which I directly afterwards found to be true; and secondly that the celebrated 'lobs' of my friend, Mr. Simpson-Hayward, the owner of the land, had no terrors for the youthful cricketers of his own village.

The many field-paths, and the welcome almost always accorded to a civil and reasonable trespasser, give a botanist searching this district a great advantage. Not that I am a botanist, nor indeed, that this bit of country is a specially interesting one botanically. But beyond doubt we have a great variety of plants, answering to the great variety of level and also of soil, to be met with in a walk from the Evenlode to the hill-tops. And though we are mere amateurs, my sister and I have both of us a great interest in flowering plants.

So I think I may venture on a few words about the floral embroidery of our neighbourhood. And I shall interpolate occasional remarks on the butterflies which adorn that embroidery; for of these insects I have known something for half a century, and they were the first living creatures to stir in me the collecting instinct. I propose to begin with the flowers of our streams, and of the alluvial meadows through which these flow: then to rise a little higher to the arable and the woodland, by which I mean not only actual wood, but well-timbered pastures: and lastly to climb to the hills, and the quarries which are here always on the tops of the hills, where good stone is to be found. Of course, the flora of these three levels overlap at all points, and many plants will be found in all three; but each has its own characteristic blooms, and the first and third are on the whole almost entirely distinct in botanical character.

Let us begin at Coxmoor. It is undoubtedly an attractive spot, for on each side of the brook there is a strip of almost level sward; on our side the grass is short and sweet, good pasture for cattle: while on the Bledington side, in another county, it is rough and tussocky, making good nesting-ground for the peewits that are here a great part of the year.

Good nesting-ground for the peewits

Before the stream itself begins to put on its floral dress, these strips are for some weeks brilliant with marsh marigolds, or kingcups, as I like to call them. In May 1911 the display was magnificent, and the rapid growth of these large-leaved plants gave the peewits a welcome cover. The great mass of bloom was on the further side, and here, too, when the kingcups faded, there suddenly broke out such a wealth of red campion as I have never seen before. It seemed as if an invisible gardener had arranged a succession of gorgeous colours, lasting from April into June.

Meanwhile the Evenlode itself had begun to display a succession of its own water-plants, each one of which gave us some botanical employment. First came the yellow flags, the bloom of which it was interesting to compare, as regards structure, with our own garden irises. Then came the yellow water lilies and with these the brilliant yellow hues, in which nature seems so greatly to delight in spring and early summer, would have come to an end, had not some creeping moneywort, and here and there a plant of St. John's wort, done their best to keep up the tradition of the earlier season. Blues and reds of various tints now began to prevail. The turquoise-blue of the forget-me-nots never fails from June to October; the water speedwell and brooklime do what they can to help, and here and there the skullcap, a really beautiful plant, shows itself, but modestly, amid the taller herbage by the brook's edge.

But the full dress of the brook is not assumed till the willow-herb and the loosestrife come into bloom. The wealth of the former was so great in 1911 as to overwhelm even the purple loosestrife. By willow-herb I mean, of course, the plant called 'codlins and cream', not the rose-bay willow-herb, which loves woods, though it is to be found close by the brook on the railway bank, blooming in September brilliantly, nor the smaller plants of the same genus, which add but little to the splendour of the stream. I suppose the very dry hot summer of last year (1911) exactly suited the constitution of the willow-herb, although I cannot explain why. I notice that particular species of the same genus will differ from one year to another in the vigour with which they grow and bloom: this year (1912) among the thistles the prosperous one is the welted thistle, which is usually a modest plant, while the marsh thistle, in most years a fine tall growth, in spite of the continued wet weather is poor and shabby-looking, even where it used to be most prominent. It is curious that a large patch of willow-herb on the Kingham brook had pure white flowers in 1911, a variation recorded by Plot in his *Natural History of Oxfordshire* as long ago as 1677. It is a plant dear to me from association with the Marsh-warbler, which sometimes found it convenient to hang its nest on the growing shoots before the bloom had come. Once, if I remember rightly, the bloom did actually come ere yet the nesting was over.

By mid-September the glory of the willow-herb had long been over, yet it left us a legacy of delicate colours, such as I cannot remember having seen before in such profusion. The prevailing tint is white, but it is faintly tinged with pink, and also with brown. The white is the result of the accumulation of winged seeds, each having silky-white hairs attached to it; the pink is the colour of the long narrow seed-vessels, and the brown is that of the dying leaves. No doubt this is why the plant is called by that pleasant nickname, codlins and cream. To see the colour in perfection you must have a sunny morning in September, when the Goldfinches are busy with the seeds, in company with the Linnets, and possibly a few Redpoles. Then the half-hour you spend by the brook can never be forgotten.

The most beautiful of all the flowers of the Evenlode is seldom seen – I mean the flowering rush. A single head of bloom appeared on the further side of the stream in this meadow last August, but some one found it out and stole it, and I looked in vain for more. I had to content myself with the greatly inferior flowers of the arrow-head and the common pondweed, which spreads its leaves so carefully and economically across the whole breadth of the stream, to give them all a fair chance of sunlight. The figwort is here, of course, attracting the wasps by the drops of honey in its corolla; for these are easy of access, and the wasps, which have only short probosces, find them a great boon. This plant is much in use in the village for burns and other sores, and my old gardener grows it in his cottage garden for such purposes, and has put one plant into mine. Much more pleasing to me is the water-mint which is now in full bloom, and deliciously scented. The teasel's upright stem and delicate lavender-bloom guarded by its fortress of needles, is abundant a little lower down the river. This year of drought (1911) it withered quickly, and its well-known stem-cups seemed to be holding but little water. In the dry hot June of 1900, at Lyme Regis, I found these cups so full of water on the dry undercliff that they would have filled my bath in a very few minutes gathering; the reason, no doubt, was the evaporation from the sea just below. While on this interesting plant, famous in the history of that industry which did so much for us as a nation, I must notice the fact that as early as the thirteenth century, and probably earlier, it was important enough to be reckoned in the parson's tithe in parishes where it grew freely. In 1221, Hugh, Bishop of Lincoln, in drawing up regulations for the new vicarages of Wycombe, Bloxham, and St. Giles (in Oxford), ordained that the vicars should have, among their other tithes, 'all tethe of tesyls that longyn to the office of fullers', which shows that the flourishing wool trade was beginning to pass into a manufacture already. Witney was, in the time of Henry III, already a town of clothiers: so we are told by the writer on Industries in the Victoria History of our county. There, and in Oxford, and other county centres, it is probable that the teasel was in demand for carding the wool; but whether in those remote times the plant used was the variety called fuller's teasel, with hooks to the bristles, afterwards specially cultivated for the purpose, or our common brookside plant, I have not been able to discover. But I must now leave the brook, just noting, before I do so, that in two spots far apart from each other, we have the wild black currant hanging over the water. I have never seen fruit on these bushes.

Above the lowest level of stream and water-meadow rises the higher ground of arable or permanent pasture, with stretches of woodland, chiefly on the Gloucestershire side of the Evenlode. The distinction between the two levels is marked in many places in a curious way; the ridges and furrows of ancient ploughing run down to within a short distance of the brook, and then suddenly end. That means that the meadows were liable to be flooded up to that point, and the ploughing necessarily stopped here, leaving a narrow strip for hay.

All these higher fields, if not ploughed, are the homes of certain abundant flowering plants which prefer not to be bred in too damp a soil. The earliest of these is my favourite the lesser celandine, the first of that long succession of 'buttercups' in which our children delight. To my thinking none of the later ones is to be compared with this either for interest or beauty. Its golden star is brighter, of a deeper gold, and larger, growing in size, indeed, as the season advances. Under favourable conditions it may break into bloom very early, though I have had to wait for it till the first days of April in this cold climate. In 1912 January was mild, and in a ditch with a steep little bank facing the midday sun, I found a bloom just showing its gold on 27th January. All through February, March, and April, these stars were still shining in the fields and hedgerows, and in some sheltered places they might be found even in the middle of May.

There is, however, an event to be looked for still earlier, which may amuse us with the happy delusion that spring is not far off; I mean the first appearance of an *arum* (lords and ladies) in some bank facing the sun. These plants sometimes fall victims to hungry thrushes, who dig them up if they are hard up for food; but otherwise they will be just appearing above ground between Christmas and New Year. They grow with wonderful speed in 'growing' weather, but sometimes they remain *in statu quo* for a month or more before they show a full green leaf. Later on they become very interesting; they develop a contrivance for cross-fertilization which is one of the easiest and most pleasing we can examine, and I showed it last spring to an eager group of our schoolboys who knew exactly where the plant was to be found in abundance, but had not penetrated its mysteries. If you can hit exactly the right week, the trap will be found which imprisons adventurous flies until the pollen falls on them, and then releases them at the right moment to carry it away to other plants.

In the spring apart from the *Ranunculaceae*, the most characteristic blooms of these pasture-fields are the cowslip and the early purple and spotted orchis. The railway embankment also abounds with cowslips. This is not a primrose country; very few primroses are to be found, even in the woods, except at Bruern, and when the church has to be decorated for Easter, the pilgrimages of depredators are all in that direction. But our light soil suits the cowslip, just as later on it suits that most beautiful of all our flowers, the large blue geranium. For geraniums in general we must go as far as Oxford, where they nearly all abound; but I must leave them for the moment till we climb to the tops of our hills.

Many field-plants are curiously local within our district; this, I suppose, is chiefly the result of the nature of the soil. In one spot, and one only, at least in the fields, we have in September the meadow saffron, which sends up a remarkable show of leaves without blooms in the spring. In one wood this plant is to be found, and there, in order to get forward to the light, it produces flower-stalks of prodigious length such as we never see in the pasture. Then in one field only near here is the beautiful thorny restharrow to be found, ruining the pasture, and apparently ineradicable, and in the next field is a single spot where I found this year that curious fern, the adder's tongue.

I notice the same local tendency of plants also in the corn-fields. The poppies, it is true, are everywhere, but the purple corn-cockle, surely one of the most beautiful of our flowers, is hardly to be found but in one field, and this year, as that field is in roots, I have not seen a single bloom. The bright blue corn-flower, an entirely different plant (for the other is a pink by descent), is commoner, but still local, and there is only one field known to me where it grows abundantly, and in the society of the yellow chrysanthemum, making a never-to-be-forgotten glory of colour in July and August. Even the little corn buttercup, a most modest retiring plant, does not seem to occur in every corn-field.

These are all beautiful flowers; but there are many in these fields that are not exactly pleasing, some that are a positive nuisance to the farmer. The tough yarrow with its head of insipid white flowers will now and then, probably as the result of some manuring of a grass field, spread itself persistently for a season. This year, 1912, which in other ways has brought so much discomfort to the farmers, has also been a happy time for their enemy the yarrow, which is tough, dull, and uninteresting, as well as harmful to the pastures. The wormwood may have a certain elegance of growth and leaf, but it is a disagreeable plant; and so, too, the various kinds of goosefoot are associated in one's mind with the dung-heaps in which they flourish. I love thistles, but the pale thistle of the arable land is not charming to my eye. More curious, but still less pleasing is the great broomrape, which occasionally pushes up its tall column of brown flowers in a field close to the village.

Before we ascend to higher levels, to the region of the old down grass and the quarries, let us look for a moment into the woods, where nothing meets the eye that is not beautiful. I think we can show such wealth of anemones and bluebells as is not easily to be outdone in any neighbourhood. Our woods are chiefly of oak, and the trunks of oaks wear, in spring, a grey lichen which harmonizes in a most wonderful way with both these flowers, first with the white, then with the blue. When these are over, a closer search may reveal less common plants, e.g. of the orchids, the twayblade, and the bird's-nest orchis, and in Bruern Wood in June the elegant white climbing fumitory. Bruern is, indeed, a good hunting-ground for botanists. I will only mention one more plant of these woods, which grows in great abundance in Churchill Heath Wood, reaching a height sometimes of eight or ten feet at least – the common marsh thistle with its sticky calyx; it is always associated in my mind with one of the most beautiful wood scenes I ever saw. One of the 'lights' in this wood was full of these tall thistles, not in themselves so very attractive to the eye; but their blooms were adorned as I have never seen them since. On each bloom there was a Silver-washed Fritillary – nay, if I recollect rightly, there were sometimes two or three on the same flower busy with the honey-glands; and he who knows that lovely insect, which is almost the most beautiful of all our British butterflies, will understand why the scene has never faded from my memory. There must have been a sudden emerging of the perfect insects, after a season peculiarly favourable to the larvae and pupae; for all were in their first glow of rich-brown above and silver-green below. The food plant is the dog violet, which, of course, abounds in this wood, and in the railway cutting adjoining it.

Now for the plants of the highest level of this region, which live in cooler and purer air and on a drier soil, and like those of the higher Alps or the chalk downs of southern England, have some peculiar charm about them that I cannot quite explain. On both sides of the Evenlode our hills run up to a height of from six to eight hundred feet above the sea; and there, even if there be but little left of the real old sheep pasture of Cotswolds or Oxfordshire Downs, we can find remnants of it in the form of broad strips of sweet grass by the road-sides, or the vegetation of a deserted quarry. It may be imagination, but when I am up here, the flowers – even those that are also found down below – seem to glow with unwonted light and harmonize with each other more perfectly. But some of them, and of the butterflies that flit about them, are peculiar to the hills. The traveller's joy is here on the hedges in abundance, but rare in the valley. The sweet violets, white, blue, and red, are far more abundant and easy to find than in the richer vegetation of the lower levels. The autumn gentian occurs and the harebell is here in its proper home, and the little white flax and the delicate dropwort, less heavily fragrant than its cousin the meadow-sweet.

The quarries are a little peculiar in their flora, and are apt to disappoint us in a dry summer like the one just past, for they absorb heat too eagerly to keep their blooms gay during a drought. A soft damp summer, with occasional sunshine, shows them at their best; and it is (or should be) a real compensation for the woes of such a season to be able to feast the eye up till October with ragwort and knapweed, scabious and poppies, and St. John's wort. Sweet thyme is here in large patches, and the pretty basil thyme, too. Among the other plants of tiny growth the scarlet pimpernel is conspicuous, and once, and only once, we found here a plant of the rarer blue pimpernel. This was in what we call 'White Quar', the nearest of these quarries, and the one out of which our village was built in successive centuries – my own house in the year 1879. I am never tired of visiting it, for the ascent in almost any weather is full of charm, not less on an autumn day like this than in the summer heat. There may be a touch of winter in my thoughts, as there is in the north-west wind that takes me in the flank; but there is much in the autumn of life to think of with pleasure, and there is much in this autumn day to look at with delight. Everywhere the fields are being ploughed, and this means in this country that uniformity of colour is giving way to variety, and dull weak yellows changing into rich reds. From the Quar I can see them ploughing in the vale below, where the field when ploughed becomes a rich chocolate, but up here on the heights there is more iron in the soil, and the land varies on a sunny day from the brightest terra cotta in the sunshine to a deep rich red in the shady hollows. The flowers of the Quar are made yet more attractive by the butterflies that flit about them. In June the Marbled Whites abound here; so too, on the Cotswold ridge opposite us they people the flowery strips of turf by the roadsides. But except on such spots you may look in vain for this delightful insect, and the grass on which its larva feeds must, I imagine, be one that is limited to the high ground. The Chalkhill Blue is another species that is here curiously limited in its range; I have seen it, so far as I can remember, only on the hill beyond Churchill, to which a lane takes off to the right, which I have named 'Butterfly lane', because these insects seem to have a peculiar delight in it. All the common kinds, which luckily include some of the most beautiful, rejoice in the upper part of this lane, and in the field to the right when you have reached the highest point – a field full of strange holes and hollows such as all butterflies delight in.

Further up beyond White Quar, near the Cross Hands Inn, there are more quarries which are the homes of almost all our most beautiful species of thistles; one of these quarries is just inside the Warwickshire border, and another has to be carried by a drive at the ninth hole of the Chastleton Golf Club. The nodding thistle abounds here – quite the most elegant of its kind, and also the great woolly thistle, whose spacious head of woolliness is attractive, but painful to handle. Here too, of course are the ground thistle and the carline thistle, and others still more common. One August when we had London children in the village, I enticed the boys up to the golf ground, thinking it would amuse them to see me play; but as they insisted on running after my ball and picking it up, I put down my clubs and gave them a lesson on thistles, in which they took a deep interest – for the moment – and as I followed it up with a bread and cheese lunch at the Cross Hands Inn, we became great friends.

Buttercups in which our children delight

Curiosities of Coxmoor

A convenient perching place near the nest

There is a certain meadow, long and narrow, with the railway as its northern and the Evenlode as its southern boundary, through which a well used footpath leads to Bledington, crossing the brook by a wooden bridge. Beyond this bridge you are as it were in a strange land; you are not only in a different parish but in a different county; you may meet labourers whom you do not know, and the farmer, if you come upon him, will behave rather as an acquaintance than a friend. Yet the sensation is not an unpleasant one; it is apt to be stimulating to the imagination. The fact that our long meadow is on the very verge of Oxfordshire, and looks across the flowery Evenlode into another long meadow in a foreign land, lends a certain charm to it which even the Yantell does not possess.

In the map of 1828, Coxmoor also appears as Coxmoor Closes and Coxmoor Flats, and I imagine that the name was suggested by the water birds which had their home here long ago in beds of sedge and reeds. The lower flat part of the meadow is liable to flood, and long ago we used to skate on it when it was both flooded and frozen; now the wettest end of it is planted with osiers, which greatly add to the attractiveness of the spot both for birds and plants and even for human beings. The foothpath to Bledington, after crossing the railway, drops down into the flat just at the corner of this osier bed, and then skirts it till it reaches the brook and the bridge. Many and pleasant are the walks beyond this bridge, on footpaths in every direction, even to the high ridge of the Cotswolds; but I wish to pause here – and indeed those long rambles are for me memories of the past – and call to mind some of the many interesting things I have seen in Coxmoor, things that send you home with curiosity awakened and a new sense of life. No other spot in all our region has given me so many pleasant surprises as this.

Even the path leading down to it from 'the Hopper' better known now as 'Jim Pearse's Cottage', has sometimes provided entertainment. I was one day pursuing my way between the hedge and the corn, and watching some Sparrows and Chaffinches that were picking up grain on the ground and then flying up to the hedge as I approached, when suddenly a Hobby shot over the hedge from behind it, dodged and twisted in the air for a moment, and then flew away towards Bledington Heath with a Chaffinch dangling from his claws. The movements of the Hobby on the wing are more wonderful, I think, than those of any other bird, for where a Hobby, or a pair of Hobbies, are sojourning for a while, they will show you their skill in flight without any shyness. When this one took his prey I was within a few yards, but he was not in the least disconcerted; yet I have known a Sparrow-hawk miss his Wheatear entirely on the crest of a Dorsetshire down, when he suddenly discovered that I was looking at him.

One hot August day some years ago I was walking slowly

down this path with the sun blazing in a cloudless sky, and wondering when I might feel the blessing of a cloud once more, when above a tall elm just beyond Coxmoor and the bridge, a quarter of a mile away, I happened to notice a cloudlike dark object. My glass showed me that it was not a distant cloud, but apparently a vast swarm of insects constantly moving; and such I found it to be when I reached the tree. As they were seventy or eighty feet above me I could not then guess what they were; but on my way home I found that all the elms had this same crown of flying creatures, and as I crossed the railway the explanation came to me. All along the railway banks there had been during the summer a most unusual number of ant-hills – hundreds of them in a very short space. From all these nests the male ants must have risen as by some pre-concerted signal, to take the one flight of their lives: or to be more correct, the queen ants must have risen all at once, and been followed by the winged males.

I happened to notice a cloud-like object

The hedge along which this path runs is a favourite haunt of both species of Whitethroat, and the loud notes of the lesser one are to be heard here each April and May, though the bird has a peculiar knack of keeping out of sight, which is provoking for a beginner who wants to see it as well as to hear. Then we come to the railway and here, just as when I wrote *A Year with the Birds*, the Whinchat builds its nest within a few feet of the rails, and sits fast while the London expresses rush past. This year a nest was shown me by a smart little boy in the school – not the one who soon afterwards discovered the three Stonechats' nests in succession, as I have already told. The nest, like all the Whinchats' nests I have ever seen here, was placed in a hole in the bank, beautifully concealed by a large leaf; but when the sun was shining it was just possible to see the blue of the eggs, if the bird were off, without descending into the ditch. Another favourite spot for the Whinchats is a little further on in Coxmoor itself, just where the path reaches the osier bed, which is fenced off by posts and rails. These birds always like to have a convenient perching place near the nest, where the cock can sing to his mate on the nest, and where the young can sit under the parents' watchful eyes as soon as they are ready to fly. Along the railway the telegraph wires serve this purpose, and here the posts and rails. One day in April some three years ago I had strolled down here looking out for the Whinchats, which had not yet arrived, and as I passed this spot they were still absent. I went on across the brook, and as I approached the place on my return I saw a little bird fly across the osiers from the south-east, and perch, not on the posts and rails, but on a high bough of an elm which stands close to this corner of the osier bed. I put up my glass to see what it could be, and found it was a cock Whinchat, which surprised me, for so far as I could remember I had never seen a Whinchat perch so high on any tree. It preened its feathers, and looked about it; and then it dawned on me that this bird was surveying, from this coign of vantage, the scene of its last summer sojourn, to make sure that there was no doubt about it, and that all was still as it should be. It is seldom indeed that one gets the chance of seeing a summer migrant actually reach its home after a journey that may have begun in central Africa.

A little further on, by the side of the brook, I once had a

curious adventure with a Partridge. I had heard shots on the rising ground on the Gloucestershire side, and saw a Partridge fly towards me and alight on my side of the brook a few feet from the water. As it remained motionless, I went towards it, but it would not stir. I walked first one side of it, then the other, passing it at about a foot's distance, without producing any effect on it. I did this once or twice, and finally touched it with my stick, when it suddenly flopped into the water, swam or shuffled across, and disappeared among the reeds on the other side. No doubt it had been hit, and felt that its best chance was to keep perfectly still. I hope it escaped after all.

But the most wonderful scenes I have ever witnessed in Coxmoor are the September gatherings of Swallows and House-martins, and chiefly of Swallows, before roosting in the osier bed. I first began to notice this in 1898 and in 1899 it was still more wonderful. On 8th September, 1898, one of the hottest days of recent times, when the thermometer at Greenwich reached 92, I found thousands of swallows circling over the osiers at a great height, and more constantly arriving, mainly from north and east. They were like gnats for multitude, and filled the still hot air with continuous sound. Suddenly there appeared among them, flying with incredible swiftness, what seemed a swallow twice or thrice the ordinary size; then another, and for some time I watched these two dashing – but this is a bad word for that marvellous and most graceful performance – through the cloud of smaller birds, which that night seemed to make no obvious effort to escape them. These swift cruisers were a pair of Hobbies, perhaps accompanying the Swallows on their journeys, in order to find a supper every evening. I did not actually see them secure a victim, but every day for a week or so I found the dead bodies of two or three swallows apparently knocked down but not devoured. I noted in my diary that the Hobbies seemed to be trying to cut off the Swallows as they descended into the osiers, which they did in zigzag fashion, as if to make it more difficult for the pirates to catch them. If the Hobbies thus kept low, the Swallows kept high, and if the Hobbies followed them up, the Swallows would descend and make for the osiers by skimming over the grass. When they flew high, the Swallows became sometimes invisible to me without the glass. The finer and clearer the weather, the higher they ascended before dropping into the osiers.

One evening I was tempted to sneak into the osiers while all these wonders were going on, and take up a position some way inside; they were then considerably higher than my head. It was a curious experience; life of the most vivid kind was all around me. A Pied Wagtail was perched on a branch close by me, and many others were about; they always used the osiers for roosting, undeterred by the multitudes of a different race. Swallows were dropping down about me, and went on chattering as soon as they had settled themselves; the place was full of sound and motion. When I started to extricate myself from this extraordinary scene there was a sudden rush of birds upwards, but they settled down again almost directly. Luckily it was an old coat that I had on for I was never able to wear it again.

For three years this performance was not repeated; the travelling hosts seemed to pass over us, and I could not discover where they found good quarters. I had by this time come to the conclusion that they must have been birds gathered together from a wide region, gaining continually in numbers till they reached the southern coast; and such vast numbers must have good thick cover to accommodate them. A well-grown or a neglected osier bed would suit them better than one in which the osiers are insufficiently grown, as ours were during those years. Then there came a year, 1902, in which, on 21st September, I found the same wonderful sight as before, but this time with a difference which was amusing. I went down at a quarter to six to see what was going on, and found some hundreds of Starlings performing their familiar evolutions; these continued till 6.5, when they all swept into the osiers and disappeared in an instant. Seeing that Swallows and Martins were collecting overhead, I remained to watch.

The numbers of the Swallow kind gradually increased until the sky became alive with them, and at about 6.20 they began to drop into the cover by twos and threes as usual. Apparently this did not please the Starlings, for in a minute or two a large detachment of them arose suddenly from the osiers, swept up among the gathering Swallows, who seemed to retreat before them – and then as suddenly descended into the cover again. It is possible that I may have been mistaken as to their motive in rising, but it was hardly possible to avoid the momentary conclusion that they wished to have the osiers to themselves. The Swallows continued to circle at a great height about the place, and the Starlings made no further movement; I saw a few Swallows slip into a corner of the osier bed, but as far as I could see the great mass of them moved on elsewhere. For a long time I could see no Hobby; but just as it was growing dusk, one passed me at incredible speed, in pursuit of some stragglers that were flying low. I continued to watch till the 30th, the show gradually diminishing in immensity and interest, and was pleased to find that the Starlings thought it as well not to be annoyed every evening after they had settled themselves down, and gradually gave up the game. This year I learnt a new fact, as the reader will have noticed; that the Starlings go to roost before the Swallows. They are ready for bed exactly at sunset, while Swallows and Martins will wait, if the weather be clear, for fully twenty minutes later. The reason no doubt is that the air is still full of insects after sunset while the Starlings have finished their feeding on the meadows long before.

I have often witnessed the roostings of the Swallows in more recent years, but have never known them so regularly pursued by Hobbies, or annoyed by Starlings. In September 1906, as I was watching them with Mr. Basil de Sélincourt, we saw a fox creep along the meadow in the growing dusk, and sneak into the osiers; but whether he proposed to himself to sup on Swallow I cannot say. The mention of this fox reminds me that another nocturnal beast of prey is not unknown in these windings of the Evenlode. The otter

hounds usually find somewhere along here, though the last
time they came they drew a blank. But a little higher up the
stream I once, in broad daylight, found a fine chub with a
large mouthful taken out of him: it looked as if the otter had
been suddenly disturbed and had left his dinner on the grass,
instead of carrying it off in his mouth.

Just where the path reaches the osier-bed, a few years ago,
a Black-headed Gull remained for about six weeks, and
contrived to pick up a living in the ooze left by floods. We
have these Gulls as visitors for a day or so occasionally,
especially in stormy weather; we are not more than thirty
miles from a tidal river. This bird was one of a small
company which had moved on, leaving their companion,
sick or injured in some way, to take its chance. It used to fly a
short way when we approached it, but soon dropped again;
strange to say, though it was for so long within a stone's
throw of a public path, no man or boy molested it, and I have
every reason to believe that it recovered and departed.

It is seldom that any other kind of Gull makes its
appearance here. But in March 1888, when after long frost
and snow the weather suddenly broke, Gulls were so
numerous at Oxford that I was on the look-out for them
here, and found both the Black-headed and the Herring
Gull, as well as two Ringed Plovers, a Dunlin, a Curlew,
(almost the only one I have seen here), endless Peewits,
Snipe getting up together in wisps, Wild Duck, Woodpigeons, Fieldfares, Redwings, Pied Wagtails, Grey Wagtails, (a pair), Meadow Pipits, Crows, Rooks, Starlings, a
Kestrel, and a Goldcrest. It is needless to say that they did
not stay long; the thaw soon reduced all fields to the same
level of public utility for the birds, which dispersed over the
country or back to the salt water of the Severn estuary.

Such are some of the curiosities of Coxmoor which are
obvious to the eye of an amateur naturalist. Many more
would in such a likely spot be revealed to the eye and mind of
a *real* naturalist. Inside that overgrown bed of osiers, for
example, how much there would be to claim the attention of
one who is at once botanist and zoologist! There comes back

upon my memory a good example, though I am just twenty years older since I came upon it.

On 19th June, 1892 my friend Aplin came over from Bloxham to see and hear the Marsh-warbler in this osier-bed. My diary tells me that we did both hear and see him satisfactorily: that we watched him singing with his bill wide open, showing a yellow 'gape' above a white fluffy throat; and that he imitated that morning the Lark, Nightingale, Thrush, Greenfinch, Black-cap, Chaffinch, Redstart, Swallow, Linnet, Yellow Wagtail, and Whinchat. My mind was therefore fully occupied, and when I passed a broken bit of rotten wood *lying on a willow leaf*, I failed to notice that such a thing was hardly possible in nature. I was a little ahead of Aplin, forcing my way through the dense cover, when I heard him say, 'Here is a pretty case of protective colouration for you.' I went back, and found that my bit of stick was a buff-tip moth in repose, with its wings rolled round its body. The moth had not taken up such a position so as to make his mimicry quite invincible; but he succeeded in taking me in. At the moment my ears were intent on the bird, to see which at that moment was impossible; and the sight of my eyes was without intelligence.

'Here is a pretty case of protective colouration for you'

A New Interest in Bird Life

This short essay, one of two on birds, was included in Essays in Brief for War-Time *which Fowler wrote in 1916: 'during the early stress of the battle at Verdun, and helped to carry me through the strain of that very critical time.'*

A man of Fowler's sensitivity, who had suffered from prolonged insomnia during the Boer War, must have been deeply troubled by the carnage and futility of the First World War. The essays, (covering a range of subjects) gave him some relief from the grief inflicted by the loss of many of the young men he had taught at Oxford and had known from babyhood in his adopted village. Characteristically, he looked to the future, when peace would enable the returning survivors to carry on the ornithological studies that had meant so much to him over the years, and were to figure in his thoughts and writing until the end of his life.

A New Interest in Bird Life

Here is work well suited to young Englishmen

All of us who have been by way of watching birds, or looking for their nests, know that many species, and especially those summer migrants which we commonly call warblers, never build their nests in close proximity to each other. Each pair seem to have a territory, a property with a couple of months' lease, where they can be sure of plenty of food for themselves and their young, and plenty of room to play in without interruption from others of their own clan. This territory (to use the word now commonly in use for the institution) may be inhabited by birds of *other* species; a Sedge-Warbler's territory in an osier-bed may also be part of the territory of a Reed-Bunting. In that case the two species live together in peace; and it may be that their food is not exactly the same, so that the most likely cause of war, except the sexual one, is eliminated. But within that territory of the

Sedge-Warbler it seems to be understood that no other
Sedge-Warbler has a right to appear.

Good examples of these territories may often be found on
the banks and in the cuttings of railways, of which some
species are particularly fond; and here they become evident
to the eye, because the birds invariably use the telegraph
wires as posts of vantage from which they can survey their
territories and the position of the nest in some hollow of the
bank below them. The railway with which I am most
familiar supplies successive pairs of Whinchats with excellent territories varying in length from one to three hundred
yards, which are only here and there broken in upon by the
claims of a Tree-Pipit or a Yellow-Hammer. In dense cover
the territories are naturally smaller, for there the pairs can
find both food and privacy in a more confined space. But I
have noticed that if the cover be cut down or if any part of it
be cleared away, the nests in the next season will be further
from each other and the territories larger. I once had under
observation, in an osier-bed of not more than half an acre, no
less than five nests of the rare marsh Warbler; but when the
greater part of the osiers were cut down, though there was
still plenty of cover that might (so we fancied) have suited
them, only one pair enjoyed this half-acre as a territory the
next season, and one or two other pairs made futile attempts
to nest in adjoining fields.

The swallow tribe, of course, have no territories, for
obvious reasons. Their food is entirely in the air, and in the
indivisible air they work and play: so they can nest in groups
or colonies without quarrelling. Gregarious birds – Rooks,
for example – need more watching before we can be sure that
they have tribal estates. But it seems to have been proved
that the flocks of Oyster-Catchers inhabiting the Firth of
Forth have clearly marked territories of sand-bank, and it
will probably be found that many other species have the
same fixed habit. To push forward our knowledge of this
'law of territory' will be much more useful work for young
and vigorous observers than bird-photography, which is
usually great waste of time.

This phrase, 'the law of territory', was invented by the distinguished ornithologist who has carried our casual knowledge of these things into the region of science, Mr. H. Eliot Howard. His conclusions may be called scientific, because they are based on knowledge collected by him in

Bird photography, which is usually a great waste of time

those hours when the birds are more full of life than at any other – the hours immediately after sunrise – and at the time of year when they are biologically more interesting than at any other – the time of courting and nesting. He rises before the sun and remains in ambush for hours: he will have nothing to do with the clumsy camera, but trusts to his pencil and his memory. When you are alone, intent on your work, eye and ear well disciplined to duty, and your interest as breathlessly keen as is possible for human nature, it is astonishing how accurate your memory can be: and if it be helped out by a kind of shorthand notes, and by rapid sketching, its evidence may be called scientific.

But it is most important that these observations should be followed up, because the conclusions based on them are still in the region of hypothesis. Clearly the 'law of territory' is of immense importance in the life of our warblers; the desire to secure a territory is what hurries on the males in front of the females during migration; their vigorous singing on arrival is an announcement of occupation, and a defiance to the claims of other males of the species: the bird's sense of boundary is unmistakable, though it may not exactly coincide with that which the observer imagines it to be.

No one can test these conclusions, and others of no less interest, who is not ready to be up with the sun when the males of a species begin to appear in their territories, and to watch and listen with eye and ear intent before the females come, during the courtship, while the nest is building, and finally during the arduous work of bringing up the family. Here is work well suited to young Englishmen who have had to accustom themselves to abnormal hours in the trenches; and work of supreme charm for those who love to be alone with other living creatures when they do not know you are watching them, and do not seem to mind you even if they find you out.

Fowler's Kingham Today

The village of Kingham retains much of the quiet charm that so appealed to William Warde Fowler on his first visit well over a century ago. Walking its streets or lingering along the many footpaths that radiate from it in every direction, it is easy, even now, to realise why he was content to settle here and why he was prompted to describe it as 'Kingham, my own home, the place of all others I love best in this world'.

From the simple grave he shares with his sister close by the church porch, inscribed:

Alice Augusta Elizabeth Fowler
Born Dec 26 1848
At Rest Jan 8 1917
William Warde Fowler
Born May 16 1847
At Rest June 16 1921

it is but a short step to the house on the corner, opposite the lych-gate, which was his first home in the village. Not far away, and unchanged externally since he built it in 1879, stands Fowler House, his home for 42 years, to which, over the years, he invited men of similar disposition, ranging from college under-graduates to eminent men of letters, to share his hospitality and walk the lonely fieldpaths in search of his beloved birds. One such visitor, Professor Julian Huxley, later recalled those days spent in Fowler's company: 'We would tramp the meadows or the hills all the afternoon, and in the midst of bird-watching or stories of birds, he would break off to tell me the history of one of the fields, or to discuss the agricultural system of Kingham in feudal times.

He was interested in the place and its history because he was unable to remain uninterested in any of the people or things with which he came into contact.'

Perhaps his favourite walk, and certainly the one which provided him with his most memorable bird experiences, was the footpath across the railway to Coxmoor and the River Evenlode. This route can still be followed today by taking the signposted track that commences beyond the village playing field opposite the church, and after passing the gardens of the council houses erected since Fowler's time, eventually crosses the Paddington-to-Hereford line into Coxmoor, a low-lying meadow through which the Evenlode picks its sluggish, meandering way.

On the left of the footpath, before reaching the footbridge that links Oxfordshire with Gloucestershire over the reedy water, can still be seen the osier bed in which Fowler observed the breeding of the marsh warbler between 1892 and 1904.

Although a considerable amount of the woodland that comprised such a significant feature of the Kingham area in Fowler's day has been cleared over the intervening years, two extensive tracts of mixed woodland remain, and thanks to the efforts of conservation bodies, are safeguarded for the future. One, a privately-owned area of woodland, is situated along the disused Chipping Norton branch line near Kingham Station; the other is the 160-acre Foxholes Nature Reserve, near Bruern, which is managed by the Berkshire, Buckinghamshire and Oxfordshire Naturalists' Trust, and along the eastern boundary of which lies the long-distance footpath, the Oxfordshire Way.

Returning to the church, the visitor cannot possibly avoid noticing the splendid building adjacent to the churchyard. This was until recently the rectory, having been built for a former incumbent, William Dowdeswell, the Elder, in 1688. In Fowler's day it was the home of Rector Samuel Davis Lockwood, preacher, fox-hunter and helper of the distressed, one of the old village characters described by Fowler in 'Kingham Old and New', and to whose memory and to 'forty years of unbroken friendship' the book was dedicated.

Nearby stands Old Rectory Cottage, formerly the home of another village character, Colonel John Barrow, who was instrumental in introducing Fowler to the village, and who was himself a competent amateur naturalist. Barrow's eccentricities are alluded to in 'A Ridge of the Cotswolds', and like Lockwood, he features prominently in 'Kingham Old and New'.

Walking along Church Street, the visitor will notice a street of new houses appropriately named 'Fowler Road' before reaching the school at the northern edge of the village, beyond the green. This building replaced the converted tithe barn which had served as a school for many years, in 1912. Fowler acted as managers' correspondent during that period and regularly visited the school, often assisting with the teaching and generally taking an interest in the children's education. Formerly an all-age establishment and now a primary school attended by the young children of Kingham and several neighbouring villages, the school has a tradition of natural history and environmental studies. Adjacent to the playground is an extensive field-study area comprising woodland, scrub and a small meadow, in the maintenance of which the children are actively involved.

The changes in the status of the wild life of the Kingham area to which Fowler referred in his writings have accelerated in the sixty-odd years since his death, attributable largely, as he himself believed, to conditions beyond the neighbourhood itself. Certain other factors, however, have clearly contributed to these changes, notably the clearing of woodland, the removal of hedges and waste, and the intensification of agricultural practice generally.

Nevertheless, the village remains a good centre for exploring several natural habitats – woodland, field and hedgerow, riverside – as well as the railway (now partly unused) to which Fowler was especially drawn. In addition, the complex of gravel pits in the Windrush valley near Bourton-on-the-Water have provided a new and rewarding source of habitat and a range of hitherto unfamiliar birds since their creation a decade or so ago.

The decline among certain bird species noted by Fowler towards the end of his life has continued steadily. The corncrake and red-backed shrike have disappeared, the yellow wagtail is a scarce passage migrant, as are the wheatear, redstart and whinchat. There is no evidence of the return of the marsh warbler. Both stonechat and nuthatch are rare in the area.

Of Fowler's other particular favourites, the grey wagtail is a fairly regular visitor, while the warblers – chiff-chaff, willow warbler, blackcap, garden warbler, sedge warbler and common and lesser whitethroat can all be found in varying degrees of abundance by the persevering enthusiast.

On the credit side, three birds – red-legged partridge, little owl and collared dove have all become well-established since Fowler's day; other species including green and greater-spotted woodpecker, goldfinch, sparrowhawk and goldcrest have reasserted themselves after earlier under-going a decline in numbers. And what, one is tempted to wonder, would Fowler make of the mixed flocks of gulls following the plough which have become a commonplace sight in recent times?

Lying as it does off the main roads and away from the celebrated tourist attractions of the nearby Cotswolds, it is easy to see why Kingham has remained relatively undis-covered to the present day. Like the writings of William Warde Fowler, the quiet scholar who knew and loved it well for almost half a century, it may be known to comparatively few, but to those so privileged it offers delights in plenty.